# GRE
## STUDY GUIDE

The Most Complete Guide to Passing the Exam on Your First Try with the Highest Score | Includes 9 Full Exam Simulations and EXTRA Weekly Exams Based on the New GRE Format

ETHAN STERLING

# TABLE OF CONTENTS

# HERE IS YOUR FREE BONUS:

## <u>Additional Full-Length Practice Test, ONE EACH WEEK</u>

Maximize your GRE test performance with exclusive, no-cost extras unlock them with the link. or the QR code provided.

Embark on the path to GRE mastery with our expertly crafted, free supplementary materials available for instant download. Tailored to enhance your comprehension and test-taking prowess, these indispensable resources are your key to attaining unparalleled preparedness.

### CLICK HERE TO DOWNLOAD IT

### OR

### SCAN THE QR CODE TO DOWNLOAD IT

# PREFACE

Beginning the journey to graduate school is a significant endeavor that demands dedication, perseverance, and a sharp intellect. The Graduate Record Examination (GRE) is a critical milestone on this journey. It serves as a universal measure of academic capability, a challenge that stands between the present and a future replete with scholarly achievement and professional growth. This book is your compass, designed to navigate the intricate landscape of the GRE.

The purpose of this guide is manifold. Firstly, it aims to demystify the GRE, presenting it not as a formidable barrier but as an opportunity to showcase the analytical and problem-solving skills honed through years of diligent study. It offers an in-depth look at each section of the exam, providing clarity on the expectations and the best approaches to meet them. Secondly, this guide equips you with strategic insights into the test's structure and content, ensuring that you understand not just what is being tested, but how and why.

This book is structured to build your understanding gradually, starting from the fundamental aspects of the GRE and advancing towards the complexities of test-taking strategies and time management. Each section of this guide is carefully crafted to address the specific challenges you will face, with practical tips and exercises that mirror the actual testing experience.

In these pages, you will find not only comprehensive reviews and practice questions but also advice on mental and physical preparation, helping you to approach the test with confidence and a clear mind. Whether you are a first-time test-taker or seeking to improve upon a previous attempt, this guide stands as a resource to refine your abilities and strategies.

As you turn each page, consider this book a testament to your commitment to excellence and a partner in your academic pursuits. Your journey to conquer the GRE begins now, and the strategies enclosed within will light your way toward success.

# CHAPTER 1: The new GRE exam

## Overview: Structure of the GRE

In September 2023, the GRE experienced a pivotal transformation. This change was implemented not just to streamline the testing process but to adapt to the evolving landscape of graduate education and the assessment of candidates' capabilities. As you prepare to undertake this examination, it's vital to familiarize yourself with its newly structured format, which retains the essence of the traditional GRE while making significant strides in efficiency

### A Comparative Look: Then and Now

Previously, the GRE was a marathon, a test of endurance as much as intellect, with a duration of nearly four hours. It encompassed two tasks in the Analytical Writing section and a total of 40 questions each in both the Verbal and Quantitative Reasoning sections. This comprehensive approach, though effective, required a substantial investment of time, both in preparation and in execution.

The current GRE, however, has been restructured to be completed in just under two hours, a reduction that speaks volumes of thoughtful redesign. The most notable change is the reduction of 46 questions combined in the Verbal and Quantitative sections, and the streamlining of the Analytical Writing section to a single task.

### Accelerated Scoring

Test-takers can now expect their official GRE results within a shorter time frame, with scores arriving in 8–10 calendar days, compared to the former 10–15 days. This expedited scoring process facilitates quicker application submissions.

### Increased Question Weight

With the reduction in the number of questions, each response now carries more weight in determining the final score. This change heightens the challenge of the exam, as each correct answer becomes even more significant.

### Elimination of Experimental Section

The experimental component, previously used for ETS research and unscored, has been removed entirely from the new GRE format. This alteration contributes significantly to the overall reduction in test duration, making the GRE a more efficient assessment.

### Dissecting the New GRE Structure

### Analytical Writing Section (AW):

The AW section, once consisting of two tasks "Analyze an Issue" and "Analyze an Argument", now focuses solely on the former. This singular 30-minute task requires a deep dive into a provided topic, demanding from you a clear, well-structured analysis grounded in rational argumentation.

### Verbal Reasoning Section (VR):

The VR section has shifted from two sections of 20 questions each to two sections of a mere 27 questions in total, with the allocated time adjusted to 41 minutes. Despite the reduction, the essence of the questions (Reading Comprehension, Text Completion, and Sentence Equivalence) remains steadfast.

### Quantitative Reasoning Section (QR):

Similarly, the QR section echoes this change. From a total of 40 questions, it now presents only 27, with 47 minutes to navigate them. The question types (quantitative comparison, problem-solving, and data interpretation) continue to challenge your mathematical prowess.

### Emphasizing Efficiency

The essence of the GRE's restructuring is not to dilute its rigor but to distill it. The reduction in the number of questions does not signify a lessening in difficulty; rather, it represents a move towards a more focused assessment of your abilities. The questions you will encounter are of the same type and quality, designed to test your analytical and critical thinking skills effectively.

### The Allocated Time: A Closer Look

In the past, the longer format necessitated a break to ensure test-takers remained sharp throughout the exam. However, with the new duration of 118 minutes, the need for an intermission has been eliminated, allowing for a more concentrated test-taking experience.

### A Modern Approach to Assessment

The GRE's new structure marks an evolution in standardized testing, one that aligns with contemporary expectations while maintaining its integrity as a comprehensive measure of readiness for graduate education. As a candidate, this translates to a less time-intensive yet equally challenging assessment. Your preparation, therefore, should be as meticulous as ever, now with the added benefit of a more concise and targeted approach to mastering the GRE.

As you utilize this book to prepare for the GRE, keep these structural changes at the forefront of your study plan. Understanding the dynamics of the new format will enable you to tailor your preparation strategies effectively, ensuring that when test day arrives, you are ready not only to meet but to exceed the expectations set before you.

# Scoring System

Navigating the scoring system of the GRE is essential for test-takers to understand how their performance translates into results. The GRE scoring system, while intricate, is designed to give graduate programs a clear picture of an applicant's capabilities. Here, we'll break down the scoring for each section and explain how it fits into the broader evaluation framework.

### Analytical Writing Scoring

The Analytical Writing section, comprising a single task since September 2023, is scored on a scale of 0 to 6, in half-point increments. Each essay is evaluated by both a human rater and a computerized program known as the e-rater. If the scores awarded by both evaluators are within one point of each other, the average becomes the final score. If there's more than a one-point discrepancy, a second human rater is brought in, and the two human scores are averaged.

This dual assessment approach ensures a balanced and fair evaluation of writing skills. The scores reflect your ability to articulate complex concepts, provide supporting evidence, and structure an argument coherently, all within the parameters of standard written English.

### Verbal and Quantitative Reasoning Scoring

The Verbal and Quantitative Reasoning sections are each scored on a scale from 130 to 170, in one-point increments, making the highest possible combined score for these sections 340. The scoring is determined by the number of questions you answer correctly, which means there's no penalty for incorrect answers. This system encourages test-takers to attempt all questions without the fear of losing points for wrong guesses.

Since the 2023 changes, the number of questions has been reduced, but the scoring scales have remained the same. Consequently, each question carries slightly more weight in the overall scoring. It's important to note that the GRE is section-adaptive at the Verbal and Quantitative levels—the difficulty of the second section is adjusted based on your performance in the first section. This adaptive feature aims to more accurately reflect a test-taker's ability at different levels of difficulty.

### Score Reporting

Your official scores for the Verbal and Quantitative sections are determined by a combination of the number of questions you answered correctly and the level of difficulty of the sections you were administered. Your official test report will provide not only your scores for each section but also percentile ranks. These ranks are particularly useful as they give context to your scores, showing how your performance compares with that of other test-takers.

### The Importance of Percentiles

Percentiles are as critical as the raw scores themselves. They help admissions committees gauge where an applicant stands in relation to peers. For instance, a percentile rank of 90 means that you scored better than 90 percent of test-takers, putting you in the top 10 percent. Programs often consider these percentiles closely when making admission decisions.

### Understanding Score Select

The GRE offers the Score Select option, which allows you to send only your best scores to the schools you're applying to. After test day, you can decide which scores from your reportable history to send to the institutions of your choice. This feature provides you with the flexibility and confidence to take the GRE more than once to achieve your best scores.

### Additional Scores and Services

Beyond the primary scores, the GRE also provides additional diagnostics, including feedback on your performance in different content areas of the Verbal and Quantitative sections. This feedback can be particularly beneficial if you plan to retake the GRE, as it can inform your study strategy and highlight areas for improvement.

### Scoring Timeline

Since the format update, GRE score reports are now generated more rapidly. Your official scores are available in your ETS (Educational Testing Service) account and sent to your selected institutions approximately ten to 15 days after your test date. The quick turnaround is advantageous for meeting application deadlines and keeping your admissions process on schedule.

The GRE's scoring system is meticulously constructed to provide a detailed and accurate portrayal of your abilities. The scores you achieve are a testament to your analytical and problem-solving skills and a key component of your graduate school application. Understanding this scoring system is crucial—not only does it help you interpret your scores, but it also guides you in setting realistic preparation goals and improving your performance for future retakes.

In essence, the GRE scoring system is as much a tool for you, the test-taker, as it is for the institutions assessing your readiness for graduate-level work.

# Test Registration and Day Tips

Registering for the GRE and preparing for test day are crucial steps in your graduate school application process. Understanding how to navigate these steps can significantly ease your test experience, whether you choose to take the exam at a test center or from the comfort of your home. This section provides detailed guidance on both registration and test day strategies, along with specific advice for both testing environments.

**Registering for the GRE**

To begin your GRE journey, you'll need to register for the test through the ETS website. ETS offers flexible scheduling options, but it is advisable to register early to secure your preferred test date and location. During registration, you can choose to take the test at a physical test center or opt for the at-home testing option, which has been made more prevalent due to increasing remote learning and assessment trends.

When registering, you will need your ETS account, where you can also access free and paid preparation materials, manage your test scores, and select institutions to send your score reports. Ensure that your identification documents are valid and match the name you use to register, as discrepancies can lead to denied entry on test day.

**Choosing Your Testing Option: Test Center vs. Home**

**Test Center:**

Taking the GRE at a test center provides a controlled environment, professionally set up to ensure an optimal testing condition. Test centers are designed to be free from distractions, with all necessary equipment provided.

Tips for Test Center Testing

- Arrive early. Get to the test center at least 30 minutes before your scheduled time to allow for check-in procedures.
- Bring your appropriate ID. Ensure your identification is valid and matches your registration details.
- Familiarize yourself with the location beforehand to avoid last-minute stress about directions.

**At-Home Testing:**

The GRE at-home testing option offers the convenience of taking the test from your own space. This option requires you to meet certain technical requirements, such as having a suitable computer, a webcam, and a reliable internet connection.

Tips for At-Home Testing

- Check your equipment. Test your computer, webcam, and internet connection using the ETS equipment check to avoid technical issues on test day.
- Prepare your testing room. Ensure your room is quiet, well-lit, and free from distractions. Your desk should be clear of all materials except for your computer and ID.
- Follow all proctor instructions. You will be monitored via webcam by a live proctor, who will guide you through the check-in process and monitor you throughout the test.

**Test Day Tips**

Whether at a test center or home, the following tips can help you approach test day with confidence:

- **Sleep well:** Aim for a full night's sleep before your test day to ensure you are rested and alert.
- **Eat a healthy meal:** Have a balanced meal before the test. Avoid heavy foods that might make you sleepy or uncomfortable.
- **Dress comfortably:** Choose comfortable clothing, considering that test centers can sometimes be cool.
- **Manage your time:** Be aware of the time limits for each section and plan your pace accordingly.
- **Take scheduled breaks:** Use the breaks to stretch, hydrate, and mentally reset.

Proper preparation for test registration and understanding the logistics of your chosen testing option can significantly influence your test performance. By following these guidelines, you can ensure that logistical issues do not detract from your focus and performance on the GRE. Whether you choose the structured environment of a test center or the familiarity of your home, being well-prepared will enable you to give your best effort.

# Test-Taking General Strategies

Approaching the GRE requires more than just a strong grasp of verbal and quantitative concepts; it demands a strategic mindset. Whether you're encountering the test for the first time or aiming to improve your score, adopting effective general strategies is crucial. These strategies are designed to optimize your study time, enhance your test-taking efficiency, and improve your overall performance. Here's a comprehensive breakdown of essential general strategies for the GRE.

### Understand the Test Format

Before you dive into studying, ensure you understand the GRE's format thoroughly. Familiarity with the structure of the test, the types of questions you will encounter, and the scoring system helps demystify the exam and reduces anxiety. Knowing what to expect can significantly bolster your confidence and improve your performance.

### Develop a Study Plan

Crafting a personalized study plan is vital. Your plan should reflect your initial diagnostic results, focusing more on areas where you need improvement while still reinforcing your strengths. Allocate specific times for studying different sections and stick to your schedule. Consistency is key; regular, disciplined study sessions are more effective than sporadic, lengthy ones.

## Practice with Purpose

Effective practice involves more than completing numerous practice questions and tests. Each practice session should have a clear objective: whether it's mastering a specific math concept or improving reading speed in verbal sections. Use quality resources that offer practice questions reflective of those on the actual GRE. After practicing, always take time to review incorrect answers to understand your mistakes fully.

## Answer Every Question

On the GRE, there is no penalty for incorrect answers, which means you should answer every question. If you're unsure about a question, eliminate as many wrong answers as possible and make an educated guess. This strategy ensures that you have a chance of scoring points on questions you might initially find challenging.

## Focus on Weaknesses, but don't Neglect Strengths

While it's important to focus on improving areas of weakness, neglecting your strengths can be detrimental. Balance is crucial; ensure that your study plan includes maintaining and refining your stronger areas to maximize your overall score.

## Learn the Art of Guessing

Sometimes, despite your best efforts, you may not know the answer to a question. Learning how to make smart guesses is an essential skill. Look for contextual clues within the question, and use logical reasoning to narrow down the choices. Often, your instinct combined with strategic elimination can guide you to the correct answer.

## Take Care of Your Well-being

A rigorous study schedule demands physical and mental stamina. Ensure you're getting enough sleep, eating nutritious foods, and taking time to relax. Regular physical activity can also boost your mental clarity. Remember, a healthy body contributes to a sharp mind, which is indispensable when preparing for a comprehensive test like the GRE.

## Simulate Real Test Conditions

As your test day approaches, simulate the testing environment: find a quiet place, set a timer, and take a full-length practice test. This strategy helps acclimate you to the pressures of the actual test day and can reduce anxiety.

## Review and Adjust

Regularly review your study and test-taking strategies to identify what's working and what isn't. Be flexible and ready to adjust your methods. If a particular approach isn't yielding improvements, try something new. Continuous adaptation is key to finding the best strategies that work for you.

By integrating these strategies into your GRE preparation, you position yourself to not only meet but exceed your test expectations. These approaches provide a robust framework that supports both your learning and performance, ensuring that you approach the GRE with confidence and well-preparedness.

# Time Management Techniques

Time management is a crucial skill for the GRE, given its comprehensive structure and the breadth of material covered. Efficient use of time can significantly influence your test scores, as it impacts both your preparation phase and your performance on test day. Here are some key time management techniques tailored specifically for maximizing your efficiency when preparing for and taking the GRE.

### Establish a Study Schedule

Creating a well-organized study schedule is the cornerstone of effective time management. Break down your preparation into manageable segments, dedicating specific blocks of time to different sections of the GRE. Allocate more time to areas where you need improvement but ensure that you also revisit your strong areas to keep them sharp. Use tools like calendars, planners, or digital apps to schedule and track your study time. Consistency is key, so aim to study at the same times each day to develop a routine.

### Set Specific Goals for Each Study Session

To make the best use of your time, set clear, achievable goals for each study session. Instead of vaguely planning to "study Verbal," decide to "complete 30 practice Verbal Reasoning questions and review explanations." This specificity helps keep you focused and makes it easier to track your progress.

### Prioritize Tasks

With the vast amount of content to cover, prioritizing tasks is essential. Tackle the most challenging topics first when your mind is freshest. Use the Pareto Principle (80/20 rule) where 20% of your focused effort gives 80% of the results. Identifying and concentrating on high-yield areas of study can make your preparation more efficient.

### Practice with Timed Sessions

Since the GRE is a timed test, integrate timed sessions into your practice. This will help you get accustomed to the pressure of working within a time limit, improving your ability to pace yourself across different sections. Start by timing each question to understand how long you take on average and gradually work on reducing this time without sacrificing accuracy.

### Use Technology Wisely

Leverage technology to enhance your time management. There are numerous apps and online tools designed to help with productivity and focus. For instance, use timer apps to keep your study sessions disciplined or use project management tools to track your preparation milestones. However, ensure that technology serves as a helper rather than a distraction.

## Develop a Test-Taking Strategy

Formulate a test-taking strategy based on your practice experiences. Determine if you perform better by quickly answering all the questions you know and then returning to harder ones, or if a more linear approach works best for you. Whichever strategy you choose, practice it consistently so it becomes second nature by test day.

## Learn to Recognize and Skip Time-Sinks

During the test, learn to recognize questions that are consuming too much time (time-sinks). If you're stuck on a question, make an educated guess, mark it for review if time permits, and move on. It's important to maintain your pace and not let a single difficult question consume the time allocated for others.

## Regular Breaks Are Essential

In both your study sessions and the actual GRE, taking regular, scheduled breaks is vital. Breaks prevent burnout and keep your mind sharp. During your preparation, take a five to ten-minute break after every hour of study. During the actual GRE, utilize the provided breaks to stretch, hydrate, and reset mentally.

## Evaluate and Adjust Regularly

Continuously evaluate the effectiveness of your time management strategies and be ready to adjust them as needed. If you find certain techniques aren't working, be flexible and try different approaches. Regular reassessment will help you find the most effective strategies for your personal style and needs.

Mastering these time management techniques will provide you with a significant advantage in preparing for and succeeding in the GRE. By optimizing how you use your time, you'll not only improve your ability to handle the exam's rigors but also enhance your overall test-taking stamina and performance. Remember, effective time management is about working smarter, not harder, and these strategies are designed to help you maximize every minute of your GRE journey.

# CHAPTER 2: Analytical Writing

## Analytical Writing Section Overview

The Analytical Writing section of the GRE stands as a critical component of the exam, designed to evaluate your ability to articulate complex ideas clearly and effectively, support arguments with logical reasoning and relevant examples, and maintain a focused and coherent discussion. This section is distinct from the Verbal and Quantitative Reasoning sections, as it assesses your writing skills rather than your ability to solve problems or understand texts. Here's a detailed overview of what you can expect from the Analytical Writing section.

**Purpose and Importance**

The primary purpose of the Analytical Writing section is to measure your critical thinking and analytical writing abilities. These skills are essential for success in graduate school, where you will be expected to produce well-structured, clear, and argumentatively sound academic writing. The ability to think critically, reason through an argument, and express your thoughts coherently is central to the demands of most graduate programs.

**Structure of the Section**

As of September 2023, the Analytical Writing section has been streamlined to include only one task: "Analyze an Issue." This modification aims to make the test shorter and less repetitive while maintaining the rigor and evaluative quality of the exam. The task requires you to write a response exploring your perspectives on a given issue. You are provided with a statement or a quotation on a topic, which you need to analyze critically and discuss the extent to which you agree or disagree with the proposed statement, supporting your views with reasons and examples.

**Duration and Setup**

The Analytical Writing section is the first part of the GRE, setting the tone for the subsequent sections. You are allocated 30 minutes to complete the "Analyze an Issue" task. This duration requires you to manage your time efficiently to plan, write, and review your essay within the given timeframe.

**Response Format**

Responses must be typed into the computer interface. Unlike traditional exams that may involve handwriting, typing responses can be advantageous as it allows for quicker editing and restructuring of your essay. You are encouraged to utilize the basic word processor provided during the exam, which permits simple cut, copy, paste, undo, and redo actions.

## Assessment Criteria

Your essay will be evaluated on several key criteria:

- **Clarity of thought and purpose:** Your ability to articulate a clear and insightful position on the issue.
- **Development of argument:** How effectively you support your position with reasons and examples.
- **Organization:** The logical flow of ideas, including the introduction, body paragraphs, and conclusion.
- **Language Use:** Your command of the English language in terms of grammar, syntax, and vocabulary.

## Preparation Tips

To prepare for this section, practice is key. Familiarize yourself with typical issue topics and practice crafting coherent and persuasive essays. Reviewing high-scoring sample essays can provide insights into effective strategies and common structures. Additionally, refining your general writing skills, such as grammar and vocabulary, is crucial.

The Analytical Writing section of the GRE, through its focus on "Analyze an Issue," offers you the opportunity to demonstrate critical thinking and sophisticated argumentative skills. It reflects your readiness for graduate-level academic challenges, making your performance in this section a vital component of your GRE results. Understanding its demands and preparing accordingly will enhance your ability to score well, providing a strong start to your GRE endeavor.

# Scoring Criteria

The scoring criteria for the GRE Analytical Writing section are meticulously designed to objectively assess your critical thinking, reasoning, and writing abilities. Understanding these criteria is essential, as it guides your preparation and practice by clarifying what the test scores are looking for in your essays. Here's a detailed breakdown of the scoring system used for the Analytical Writing section, which involves evaluating your ability to analyze an issue effectively.

## Fundamental Aspects of Scoring

The Analytical Writing section is scored on a scale from 0 to 6, in half-point increments. This score is derived from the assessments made by both human raters and a specialized computer program developed by ETS known as the e-rater. Each essay is first scored independently by a trained human rater and then by the e-rater. If the scores from the human and the e-rater are close, the average of these scores becomes your final score for the task. If there is a discrepancy of more than one point between the scores, a second human rater evaluates the essay, and the final score is the average of the two human scores.

## Criteria Used by Human Raters

Human raters are trained to evaluate essays based on several key dimensions:

- **Quality of ideas:** This measures the depth and complexity of the ideas and examples used. High-scoring essays feature insightful, nuanced considerations of the issue with relevant, persuasive examples supporting the arguments.
- **Logical development and organization:** This includes the clarity of your thesis (or main idea) and the logical sequence of arguments that support your thesis. Effective transitions, clear topic sentences, and a logical progression of ideas from the introduction to the conclusion are essential.
- **Clarity and command of standard written English:** Essays must be not only grammatically correct but also stylistically clear. This aspect involves proper use of vocabulary, variety in sentence structure, and overall fluency that enhances the readability and impact of your argument.

## Criteria Used by the e-rater

The e-rater, designed to complement human judgment, evaluates essays based on linguistic and structural features that reflect effective writing:

- **Syntactic variety and complexity:** The e-rater analyzes the range and complexity of sentence structures in your essay, rewarding those that demonstrate syntactic variety and sophistication.
- **Usage and mechanics:** This part includes grammar, spelling, and punctuation. The software checks for common errors and the correct use of standard written English conventions.
- **Vocabulary usage:** The software evaluates the appropriateness and complexity of vocabulary used in the essay. Effective use of vocabulary enhances the clarity and precision of your essay.
- **Discourse structure:** The e-rater assesses the organizational structure of your essay, including the presence and effectiveness of an introduction, body paragraphs, and a conclusion. It also looks for cohesive elements like transitions and connectives that help the flow of the essay.

## Relevance of the Scoring Criteria

The scoring criteria are designed to reflect the level of analytical writing and critical thinking expected in graduate and business schools. The emphasis on logical argumentation, clarity of expression, and effective language use mirrors the skills necessary for academic success in demanding programs.

## Preparation Based on Scoring Criteria

To prepare effectively for the Analytical Writing section and meet these criteria, focus on the following during your practice:

- **Develop a clear argument:** Always make sure your essay has a clear position on the issue, supported by logically reasoned arguments.
- **Practice writing coherent and cohesive essays:** Work on structuring your essays in a way that each paragraph naturally flows to the next, with clear transitions.
- **Enhance your vocabulary:** A richer vocabulary allows for more precise and impactful communication.
- **Regular feedback:** Regularly get your practice essays evaluated by others, or use online tools that simulate the e-rater's feedback, to improve based on the scoring dimensions.

By understanding the detailed scoring criteria for the GRE Analytical Writing section, you can tailor your preparation strategy to align closely with what is valued most in your essays. This alignment not only improves your potential scores but also enhances your overall analytical writing skills, paving the way for academic and professional success in the future.

# Strategies for the Analyze an Issue Task

The "Analyze an Issue" task tests your ability to think critically about a topic of general interest and to express your thoughts about it in writing. Each Issue task statement presents a claim or assertion on a topic that requires you to take a position and support it with reasons and examples. Understanding the nuances of this task is crucial for effective preparation and success.

### Purpose of the Issue Task

The primary goal of the Issue task is to assess your ability to engage with complex ideas, develop an argument, and communicate effectively through writing. Unlike the Argument task, which asks you to evaluate someone else's argument, the Issue task requires you to build your own argument from scratch. It's your opportunity to demonstrate your critical thinking, reasoning, and persuasive writing skills.

### Structure of the Task

The Issue task begins with a brief statement about a topic, which can range from the arts and sciences to business and education. The statements are intentionally broad and can be approached from multiple perspectives. Following the statement, you will typically find instructions on how to frame your response. These instructions are crucial as they guide the scope and angle of your argument.

### Key Components of the Issue Task

### 1. Analyzing the Statement

Start by carefully reading the statement to fully understand what it's asking. Identify the central claim or assumption in the issue statement. This understanding forms the basis of your response.

## 2. Choosing a Position

Decide whether you agree, disagree, or take a nuanced position relative to the statement provided. There is no "right" answer; the quality of your essay depends on how well you support your position with reasoning and examples.

## 3. Developing Your Argument

Once you've chosen your stance, think critically about the reasons that support your position. Develop a list of main points and examples that substantiate your view. These can come from your own experiences, historical examples, current events, or scientific studies, among others.

## Planning Your Response

Effective planning is key to a successful Issue essay. Allocate a few minutes at the start to outline your essay. This outline should include:

- **Introduction:** Briefly paraphrase the issue statement and clearly state your position.
- **Body paragraphs:** Each paragraph should focus on a single main point. Start with a topic sentence that introduces the point, followed by an explanation and examples that substantiate it.
- **Conclusion:** Summarize your argument and reinforce your position succinctly.

## Writing Your Essay

When writing, focus on clarity and coherence. Use a formal, academic tone and precise language. Ensure that each paragraph logically flows into the next. Transitions between paragraphs are particularly important as they contribute to the overall coherence of your essay.

## Time Management

The Analytical Writing section gives you 30 minutes to complete the Issue task. Managing this time effectively is critical:

- Spend about five minutes planning.
- Around 20 minutes should be devoted to writing the essay.
- Use the last five minutes to review your essay and make any necessary revisions.

## Common Challenges and Strategies

- **Overgeneralization:** Avoid making sweeping generalizations in your arguments. Be specific in your examples and reasoning.
- **Time pressure:** Practice timed essays to get comfortable with the 30-minute limit.

- **Topic familiarity:** While you won't know the topic beforehand, familiarizing yourself with common themes can help you prepare examples and ideas that can be adapted to various issues.

Mastering the Issue task on the GRE Analytical Writing section demands not only good writing skills but also the ability to think critically and argue effectively. Understanding the task's requirements, practicing extensively, and being mindful of your argumentative strategies are key to producing a compelling and thoughtful essay. With thorough preparation, you can approach this task with confidence, ready to showcase your analytical abilities and writing prowess.

# Structuring Your Response

The structure of your response in the "Analyze an Issue" task is pivotal for conveying your argument effectively. A well-organized essay not only makes it easier for the reader to follow your thoughts but also enhances the persuasiveness of your argument. Understanding how to structure your response is essential for scoring well on this part of the GRE Analytical Writing section.

**Importance of Structure**

The structure of your essay impacts its clarity, coherence, and overall persuasiveness. A clear structure helps you maintain focus, guiding the reader through your arguments logically and systematically. It also ensures that each part of your essay contributes toward the overall thesis, reinforcing your position with each paragraph.

**Basic Essay Structure**

A strong GRE essay typically follows a classic five-paragraph format, which includes an introduction, three body paragraphs, and a conclusion. This format serves as a reliable template for presenting a well-rounded argument.

*1. Introduction*

- **Opening sentence:** Start with a hook—a compelling statement or question that grabs the reader's attention.
- **Thesis statement:** Clearly state your position on the issue. This one is a critical component as it sets the direction for the rest of your essay.
- **Brief outline:** Optionally, you can briefly mention the main points that will support your thesis. This helps in setting expectations and gives the reader a roadmap of your essay's structure.

*2. Body Paragraphs*

Each body paragraph should focus on a single point that supports your thesis. The ideal structure for each body paragraph includes:

- **Topic sentence:** Open with a sentence that introduces the main idea of the paragraph.
- **Explanation:** Explain the relevance of this idea and how it supports your thesis.
- **Evidence:** Provide specific examples, data, or anecdotes that substantiate your point. These could be drawn from scholarly sources, reputable news outlets, historical events, personal experiences, or hypothetical scenarios.
- **Link back:** Conclude the paragraph by linking the discussion back to the thesis, reinforcing how this point supports your overall argument.

### 3. Conclusion:

- **Summary:** Briefly recap the main points made in your body paragraphs, summarizing how each contributes to supporting your thesis.
- **Restatement of thesis:** Reinforce your thesis, now that you've demonstrated its validity through your body paragraphs.
- **Closing thought:** End with a strong closing statement. It could be a call to action, a rhetorical question, or a prediction about the implications of your argument. This is your last chance to leave a lasting impression on the reader.

## Advanced Structural Techniques

While the five-paragraph essay is a safe and effective structure, you can employ more sophisticated organizational strategies as you become more comfortable with the task:

- **Counterargument:** Consider dedicating a paragraph to addressing a counterargument. This demonstrates critical thinking and confidence in your position by acknowledging and refuting opposing views.
- **Thematic organization:** Instead of structuring paragraphs by points, organize them around themes or questions that explore different dimensions of the issue.

## Practical Tips for Structuring Your Essay

- **Plan before you write:** Spend the first few minutes planning your essay. Jot down your main points and examples on scratch paper. This planning phase ensures that your essay remains focused and doesn't stray off-topic.
- **Be flexible:** While it's good to start with a plan, be flexible. As you write, you might find some points require more emphasis or that your argument is evolving slightly. Adjust your structure as needed while maintaining overall coherence.
- **Transitions:** Use transitional phrases to connect ideas between paragraphs smoothly. Phrases like "Furthermore," "However," "In addition," and "As a result" help maintain the flow of your essay.

The structure is more than just a skeleton for your essay; it's the framework that supports and enhances your argument. By mastering the art of structuring your responses on the GRE's "Analyze an Issue" task, you can significantly boost the clarity and effectiveness of your writing, thereby improving your chances of achieving a high score. Practice diligently, employing these structuring techniques, and with time, organizing your thoughts in a clear, logical manner will become second nature.

# Practice Prompts with Sample Essays

One of the most effective ways to prepare for the GRE Analytical Writing section's "Analyze an Issue" task is to practice with sample prompts. This practice not only helps you familiarize yourself with the types of issues you might encounter but also enables you to see how well-structured responses are developed. This section provides detailed information on how to utilize practice prompts effectively and includes sample essays to illustrate key strategies in action.

### Benefits of Using Practice Prompts

Practice prompts serve several essential functions in GRE preparation:

- **Familiarity:** They help you become accustomed to the format and phrasing of typical GRE issues, reducing surprises on test day.
- **Skill development:** Regular practice with these prompts enhances your ability to think critically and articulate your thoughts under timed conditions.
- **Feedback and improvement:** By writing practice essays, you can receive feedback on your writing from instructors or peers, allowing you to identify areas for improvement.

### Selecting Practice Prompts

ETS, the organization that administers the GRE, provides a pool of Issue tasks on its official website. These are actual prompts that have been used in past GRE tests and are excellent resources for practice. When selecting prompts:

- **Variety:** Choose prompts that cover a range of topics and positions to ensure you're well-prepared for any issue.
- **Relevance:** Occasionally, certain themes may be more prevalent. Keeping abreast of current academic and social discussions can help in choosing the most pertinent prompts.

### Structure of a Practice Session

When practicing with these prompts, structure your session to mimic actual test conditions as closely as possible:

- **Timing:** Allocate 30 minutes to complete each essay. This helps build your time management skills.

- **Environment:** Practice in a quiet, test-like environment to simulate the conditions you will face during the actual test.
- **Review:** After writing, spend time reviewing your essay critically. Assess it against the scoring criteria provided by ETS and consider areas for improvement.

## Sample Essay Response

**Prompt:** "In any field of endeavor, it is impossible to make a significant contribution without first being strongly influenced by past achievements within that field."

## Sample Essay

### Introduction

In the pursuit of innovation and contribution within any field, the significance of historical context cannot be overstated. This essay argues that past achievements are not merely influential but indeed foundational to future contributions in any domain.

### Body Paragraph 1

Historical achievements provide a framework upon which contemporary work is built. For instance, in the field of science, the discovery of DNA's double-helix structure by Watson and Crick has been fundamental to advancements in genetics. Without this foundational knowledge, modern genetic engineering would not be feasible.

### Body Paragraph 2

Moreover, past achievements inspire current and future generations to push boundaries and expand existing knowledge. The accomplishments of pioneers like Marie Curie in radioactivity or Steve Jobs in technology serve as powerful motivators for aspiring scientists and entrepreneurs. Their legacies demonstrate what is possible, encouraging others to innovate further.

### Body Paragraph 3

Acknowledging the influence of past achievements does not diminish the value of new contributions. Rather, it highlights the cumulative nature of knowledge and progress. Each generation adds to the body of work left by its predecessors, creating a richer tapestry of human achievement.

### Conclusion

Contrary to the view that original contributions can stand alone, this essay posits that all significant endeavors are built on a rich heritage of past achievements. The influence of historical milestones is not just an influence but a necessity, providing the tools and inspiration necessary for future innovations.

## Analyzing the Sample Essay

The provided sample essay showcases:

- **Clear structure:** Introduction, body paragraphs, and a conclusion that neatly ties the argument together.
- **Direct address of the prompt:** It directly responds to the prompt's statement and develops an argument around it.
- **Use of examples:** Specific examples from varied fields illustrate the argument.
- **Cohesiveness and coherence:** The essay flows logically from one paragraph to the next, with each point building on the previous one.

Using practice prompts with sample essays is a critical part of your GRE preparation. They not only improve your writing skills but also enhance your ability to think critically under timed conditions. By studying sample essays, you can learn effective strategies to structure your responses, making your writing more coherent and compelling. Through diligent practice, you can master the art of crafting persuasive essays that stand out in the GRE Analytical Writing section.

# CHAPTER 3: Verbal Reasoning

## Verbal Reasoning: Types of Questions

The Verbal Reasoning section of the GRE is designed to test your ability to analyze and evaluate written material and synthesize information obtained from it, analyze relationships among component parts of sentences, and recognize relationships among words and concepts. Understanding the types of questions, you will encounter in this section is crucial for effective test preparation and success. Here's a detailed look at the various types of questions that make up the Verbal Reasoning section of the GRE.

### Reading Comprehension

#### Description

Reading Comprehension questions measure your ability to understand, analyze, and apply information and concepts presented in written form. This type of question typically presents a passage followed by a set of questions that ask about the content, assumptions, implications, or structure of the passage.

#### Types

- **Multiple-choice questions (single answer):** These questions require you to select one correct answer from a list of options.
- **Multiple-choice questions (multiple answers):** These questions allow you to choose more than one answer. Points are awarded only if all correct choices are selected, with no partial credit given.
- **Select-in-passage:** You are asked to click on the sentence in the passage that best answers a specific question.

### Text Completion

#### Description

Text Completion questions test your ability to use contextual clues to complete a passage with blanks from a list of possible options. Each blank has three answer choices, and you must select the one that best fits the context of the passage.

#### Types

- **Single-blank:** Short passages with one blank to fill.

- **Double-blank:** Passages with two blanks, each needing the correct word choice that fits the overall meaning of the passage.
- **Triple-blank:** More complex passages with three blanks, testing your ability to evaluate how different parts of the passage relate to one another.

## Sentence Equivalence

### Description

Sentence Equivalence questions measure your ability to reach a conclusion about how a passage should be completed on the basis of partial information, but also to recognize how different words or phrases can be used interchangeably to maintain the same meaning in a sentence.

### Types

- **Single sentence:** You are given a single sentence with one blank and you must choose two answers from a list of six choices that give the sentence a similar meaning when inserted into the blank.

## Strategies for Answering Verbal Reasoning Questions

### 1. Contextual Reading

For all types, it is vital to read the context provided carefully. Whether it's a passage or a sentence with a blank, understanding the overall tone, purpose, and direction of the text is crucial for selecting the correct answer.

### 2. Vocabulary Knowledge

A strong vocabulary helps immensely, especially with Text Completion and Sentence Equivalence questions. Knowing the subtle nuances of similar words can be the key to selecting the correct answers.

### 3. Critical Thinking

Especially for Reading Comprehension, being able to analyze the text critically—identifying the author's tone, assumptions, and conclusions—is necessary for answering the questions correctly.

### 4. Practice and Review

Regular practice with different types of verbal reasoning questions is essential. After practicing, always review your answers and understand why certain choices were correct or incorrect to improve your performance.

Familiarizing yourself with the types of questions in the Verbal Reasoning section of the GRE enables you to tailor your study strategy accordingly. By understanding the demands of each type and regularly practicing, you can enhance your verbal reasoning skills, ultimately leading to better performance on test day.

# Question Strategies

To excel in the Verbal Reasoning section of the GRE, it is essential to employ specific strategies tailored to the structure and demands of this section. Effective question strategies can help you efficiently manage time, avoid common pitfalls, and maximize your score. Here's a detailed guide on approaches to adopt for each type of question you will encounter in the Verbal Reasoning section.

## General Strategies for All Question Types

### 1. Read Actively

Engage actively with the text, whether it's a long passage or a single sentence. Make mental notes or quick annotations about the main idea, tone, and structure. Active reading helps in faster recall and clearer understanding, essential for answering questions accurately.

### 2. Manage Time Wisely

Allocate your time based on the type of question. Reading Comprehension questions might require more time compared to Text Completion due to the length of passages. Practice pacing yourself to ensure you have adequate time to address all questions without rushing.

### 3. Prioritize Easy Questions

Quickly move through the test to answer questions you find straightforward first. Mark more challenging questions and return to them after securing all the easier points. This ensures that difficult questions do not monopolize your time.

## Strategies for Reading Comprehension

### 1. Skim First

Before diving into the questions, skim the passage to get a general sense of the content and structure. Identify the main argument and note any shifts in tone or topic. This initial overview guides where to look for answers when you tackle specific questions.

### 2. Focus on Keywords in Questions

Pay close attention to keywords in questions and answer choices. Words like "except," "not," or "only" are critical since they define the scope of the correct answer. This helps in quickly eliminating incorrect options.

### 3. Use the Process of Elimination

Especially useful in difficult questions where more than one answer might seem correct. Cross out answers that are clearly wrong, then focus on distinguishing between the remaining choices by finding subtle differences or textual evidence.

## Strategies for Text Completion

### 1. Fill in Blanks Without Looking at Choices

Try to fill in the blanks with your own words before looking at the answer choices. This activity helps in predicting the type of word that fits, making it easier to spot the right answer among the choices.

### 2. Evaluate Each Blank Independently

If there are multiple blanks, treat each independently to prevent confusion and allow you to focus on finding the best fit for each context.

### 3. Check for Overall Coherence

After filling in the blanks, read the completed sentence or passage to ensure it flows logically and coherently. This action helps in catching any inconsistencies you might have overlooked.

## Strategies for Sentence Equivalence

### 1. Identify Clues in the Sentence

Look for clues within the sentence that hint at the meaning or context required by the blank. These could be contrast words like "however," or continuation words like "moreover."

### 2. Look for Synonymous Pairs

Since you need to find two words that yield similar meanings when inserted in the blank, focus on identifying pairs among the choices. Dismiss words that don't have a clear counterpart.

### 3. Double-check Both Fit

After selecting what seems like a pair, insert each into the sentence to ensure both work independently. They should both fit seamlessly without altering the overall meaning of the sentence.

Mastering these strategies requires practice and attentiveness to the nuances of the test format and types of questions. By implementing these targeted approaches, you can enhance your performance in the Verbal Reasoning section, optimizing both your efficiency and effectiveness. Remember, each strategy aims to reduce the cognitive load during the test, allowing you to focus on demonstrating your verbal skills to the fullest.

# Reading Comprehension: Techniques for Effective Reading

Reading comprehension on the GRE involves more than just reading the words on the page, it requires a deep understanding and analysis of the text. Effective reading techniques can significantly enhance your ability to interpret complex passages and answer questions accurately. Here's a detailed guide on strategies to improve your reading comprehension for the GRE.

## Develop Active Reading Habits

### 1. Preview the Text

Before you dive into detailed reading, quickly skim the passage to get a sense of the main topic, structure, and tone. Look at headings, if any, and the introductory and concluding sentences of paragraphs. This initial overview provides a framework for understanding the detailed information to follow.

### 2. Ask Questions

As you read, ask yourself questions about the text. What is the main argument? What evidence does the author use? What are the implications of this argument? Asking questions keeps you engaged and often helps predict what might be asked in the questions that follow.

### 3. Annotate and Summarize

Make brief notes as you read, annotating key points, unfamiliar terms, and any conclusions you draw from the material. Summarize paragraphs in the margins to reinforce understanding and retention. This practice is particularly useful for long and complex passages.

## Focus on Structure

### 1. Identify Structural Keywords

Pay attention to words and phrases that signal structure, such as "however," "for example," and "consequently." These keywords can help you understand how ideas are connected and structured, which is crucial for answering questions about the author's argument and the organization of the passage.

### 2. Understand Paragraph Roles

Each paragraph typically serves a specific role in advancing the overall argument. Try to identify the purpose of each paragraph—whether it's introducing an idea, providing evidence, or offering a counterargument. This understanding can quickly help you locate information when answering questions.

## Enhance Vocabulary

### 1. Contextual Vocabulary Learning

Instead of rote memorization, focus on learning vocabulary in context. This approach helps you understand not only what words mean but also how they are used in sentences, which is essential for Text Completion and Sentence Equivalence questions.

### 2. Use a Vocabulary Journal

Keep a journal of new words you encounter in your reading. Note the definition, synonyms, and an example sentence for each word. Regular review of this journal can enhance your vocabulary retention and recall.

## Improve Information Retention

### 1. Develop Concentration

Reading comprehension requires a high level of concentration. Practice reading in environments free from distractions. Gradually increase your reading sessions to build your concentration stamina, which is crucial for the long passages on the GRE.

### 2. Recitation Technique

After reading a section, pause and try to recite the main ideas and details. This technique reinforces memory retention and ensures you have a firm grasp of the text.

## Practice Analytical Reading

### 1. Evaluate the Argument Critically

Beyond understanding what the text says, assess the strength of the argument. Evaluate the evidence provided, identify any biases or assumptions, and consider what information might be missing. This critical approach is essential for handling complex passages on the GRE.

### 2. Practice with Diverse Materials

To prepare for the variety of passages on the GRE, practice reading from diverse sources and disciplines: science, arts, humanities and social sciences. This exposure will familiarize you with different writing styles and terminologies.

Mastering reading comprehension for the GRE involves cultivating a set of skills that go beyond simple reading. By employing these techniques, you can enhance your understanding of complex texts, improve your ability to recall and analyze information, and increase your overall test performance. Regular practice, combined with a strategic approach to reading, will equip you with the tools necessary to excel in the Reading Comprehension section of the GRE.

# Practice Passages with Questions

To excel in the Reading Comprehension section of the GRE, it is essential to engage with a variety of practice passages accompanied by questions. These practice exercises are crucial for honing your reading strategies, enhancing your understanding of complex texts, and improving your ability to answer questions accurately under timed conditions.

Work with passages that vary in length and complexity to build your adaptability. Longer passages can help improve your stamina and concentration, while shorter passages can aid in quick information retrieval and analysis.

## 1. Global Questions

These questions ask about the main idea, theme, or purpose of the entire passage. Practice identifying the author's primary purpose and the main thesis of the text.

## 2. Detail Questions

These require you to locate or infer details from the passage. Enhance your ability to scan for factual information and understand implications or subtleties within the text.

## 3. Inference Questions

These questions ask you to draw conclusions based on information not explicitly stated. Practice reading between the lines and using evidence from the text to support your inferences.

## 4. Vocabulary-in-Context Questions

These ask about the meaning of a word or phrase within the context of the passage. Focus on understanding how words function in sentences to determine their meanings rather than relying solely on prior vocabulary knowledge.

### Strategies for Answering Questions

## 1. Elimination Technique

For all types of questions, use the process of elimination to narrow down your choices. Discard answers that are clearly wrong to improve your chances of selecting the correct response.

## 2. Refer Back to the Passage

Always validate your answers by referring back to the passage. This practice ensures that your answers are grounded in the text and not based on assumptions or external knowledge.

## 3. Manage Time

Allocate time proportionally based on the length and complexity of the passage and the number of questions associated with it. Practice pacing yourself to ensure that you can comfortably handle both long and short passages within the allotted time.

**Review and Reflect**

*1. Review Answers*

After completing a set of questions, carefully review both your correct and incorrect answers. Understand why an answer is right or wrong, and analyze any patterns in the mistakes you make.

*2. Reflect on Strategies*

Reflect on the reading and answering strategies you used. Determine what worked and what didn't, and adjust your approaches accordingly for future practice.

Utilizing practice passages with questions is a dynamic way to prepare for the GRE Reading Comprehension section. By systematically working through diverse and challenging texts, you not only improve your reading and analytical skills but also enhance your test-taking strategies, ensuring you are well-prepared to excel in the actual exam. Regular practice, combined with thoughtful review and reflection, is the key to mastering the Reading Comprehension section of the GRE.

# Tips for Answer Accuracy

Achieving accuracy in the Reading Comprehension section of the GRE is crucial for a high verbal score. This part of the test assesses your ability to understand and interpret written material, and answering questions accurately requires both strategic reading and critical thinking. Here are essential tips to enhance your accuracy in answering Reading Comprehension questions on the GRE.

**Develop a Systematic Reading Strategy**

*1. Active Reading*

Engage actively with the text as you read. This means not just reading the words but thinking about what the author is trying to communicate. Ask questions, make predictions, and summarize passages in your own words.

*2. Skimming and Scanning*

Learn to skim for general understanding and scan for specific information. Skimming helps you grasp the main idea and structure of the passage, while scanning is useful for locating specific details to answer questions accurately.

### 3. Annotate Strategically

While practice reading, make brief annotations or notes that capture the essence of paragraphs or highlight critical pieces of information. This practice can help you quickly locate information during the exam and check the details needed for answering specific questions.

## Understand Question Types and Tactics

### 1. Main Idea Questions

For questions that ask for the main idea or primary purpose, focus on the introduction and conclusion, as these often contain the core argument or summary. Be wary of answer choices that are too broad or too specific.

### 2. Detail Questions

These require you to identify specific information stated in the passage. Always go back to the passage to confirm the details before choosing an answer. Trust only the information provided in the text, not your assumptions or external knowledge.

### 3. Inference Questions

Approach inference questions by evaluating the logical implications of the passage's content. Avoid extreme answer choices that make broader generalizations than the text supports. Use elimination to discard clearly incorrect answers.

### 4. Vocabulary in Context

When asked about the meaning of a word in context, consider how the word functions in the sentence. Look at the sentences around it for clues about its meaning, rather than relying solely on a predefined definition.

## Timing and Pacing

### 1. Allocate Time Wisely

Balance your time between reading and answering questions. Although it's important to read thoroughly, spending too much time on reading leaves less time for answering questions. Practice pacing to find a balance that works for you.

### 2. Prioritize Questions

Answer easier questions first to secure quick points, then return to more challenging ones. This ensures that you don't miss out on scoring opportunities while stuck on difficult questions.

## Review Techniques

### 1. Cross-Verification

Before finalizing an answer, verify it by cross-checking with the passage. This double-checking process can prevent mistakes due to misreading or overlooking crucial information.

### 2. Review Wrong Answers

When practicing, spend time reviewing not just the questions you got wrong but also those you were unsure about, even if you guessed them right. Understand why the correct answers are right and why the wrong options are not suitable.

## Enhance Test-Taking Stamina

### 1. Build Reading Stamina

Increase your reading stamina by gradually lengthening your practice sessions. Start with shorter passages and work your way up to longer or more complex ones, mirroring the test conditions.

### 2. Practice Under Timed Conditions

Regularly practice under timed conditions to accustom yourself to the pressures of the test. This helps in managing time effectively during the actual exam.

Improving answer accuracy in the Reading Comprehension section involves a combination of effective reading strategies, understanding question types, strategic practice, and careful review. By incorporating these tips into your preparation, you can enhance your ability to interpret questions correctly and select the most accurate answers, ultimately boosting your performance on the GRE.

# Text Completion: Solving Text Completion Questions

Text Completion questions on the GRE Verbal Reasoning section challenge test-takers to demonstrate their ability to interpret, evaluate, and complete sentences and passages based on the information provided. These questions are designed to assess vocabulary strength, reading comprehension, and the ability to use contextual cues to make logical connections. Here are strategies to effectively approach and solve Text Completion questions.

## Understand the Basics

Text Completion items consist of a passage with one to three blanks, and for each blank, you are given three choices. Your task is to select the word or phrase that best completes the text based on the overall meaning of the sentence or passage. Single-blank items test your vocabulary directly, while two- or three-blank items require more integration of information and assessment of how different parts of the sentence relate to each other.

**Step-by-Step Approach**

*1. Read the Sentence Carefully*

Before looking at the answer choices, read the sentence or passage thoroughly to understand its overall content and tone. Try to get a sense of what the author is discussing and the direction of the statement or argument.

*2. Predict the Answer*

Before you look at the available choices, try to fill in the blank(s) with your own answer based on the context of the sentence. This method helps prevent preconceived biases towards the provided options and sharpens your focus on the text's requirements.

*3. Analyze Contextual Clues*

Look for keywords or phrases in the sentence that indicate contrast (e.g., however, although), addition (e.g., moreover, furthermore), or cause and effect (e.g., because, thus). These clues can help you understand the relationship between different parts of the sentence and predict what kind of word is needed.

*4. Evaluate Each Option*

Consider each answer choice independently within the context of the blank. Insert each option into the blank and decide if it makes sense both grammatically and logically. Be wary of words that seem to fit the sentence structurally but alter the intended meaning or tone.

**Dealing with Multiple Blanks**

For sentences with multiple blanks, the complexity increases as the blanks often depend on one another for cohesive meaning:

- **Start with the easiest blank:** Sometimes, one blank will be easier to fill than the others. Start there, as filling in one blank can provide additional context that makes solving the remaining blanks easier.
- **Check for consistency:** Once you have selected words for each blank, read the complete sentence to ensure that all the words work together to form a coherent statement. Each part should logically follow from the others, and the overall sentence should make sense.

**Common Pitfalls to Avoid**

*1. Misreading the Tone or Logic*

A common mistake is missing the overall tone or logical flow of the sentence. Pay close attention to whether the sentence is building towards a particular conclusion or making a contrastive point.

*2. Overreliance on Vocabulary*

While a robust vocabulary is crucial, relying solely on word recognition without considering context can lead to errors. Always integrate your vocabulary knowledge with contextual analysis.

### 3. Ignoring Part of Speech

Sometimes the correct answer is simply about recognizing the right part of speech that fits the blank grammatically. Be alert to these grammatical cues.

### Practice Regularly

Practice is key to mastering Text Completion questions. Regularly engage with practice questions from reliable sources, such as official GRE preparation materials. After completing practice questions, review your answers to understand why certain choices were correct and why others were not. This reflection will deepen your understanding and improve your ability to choose wisely under exam conditions.

Effectively solving Text Completion questions requires a blend of sharp reading skills, contextual understanding, and vocabulary knowledge. By employing these strategies, you can enhance your ability to dissect complex sentences and fill in the blanks accurately, significantly boosting your performance in the Verbal Reasoning section of the GRE.

# Practice Questions

To excel in the Text Completion section of the GRE Verbal Reasoning test, regular practice with well-crafted questions is essential. This practice helps you develop the necessary skills to analyze sentences and longer passages efficiently, choose appropriate words or phrases to complete a text, and understand the nuances of vocabulary and context. Here's how to effectively use practice questions to enhance your preparation.

### Selecting High-Quality Practice Questions

### 1. Source Reliable Materials

Always choose practice questions from reputable sources, such as official ETS materials, well-reviewed test prep books, or respected online platforms. High-quality questions mimic the style and difficulty level of the GRE, providing a realistic practice experience.

### 2. Variety in Difficulty and Structure

Ensure your practice includes a mix of question difficulties and structures. Some questions should have single blanks, while others should have two or three, which require you to juggle multiple contextual clues simultaneously.

### Effective Techniques for Practicing Text Completion

## 1. Read Thoroughly Before Answering

Read the sentence or passage without looking at the answer choices to avoid being influenced by them. Try to fill in the blanks with your own words based on what logically and stylistically fits.

## 2. Analyze the Context

Focus on the overall meaning of the sentence or passage. Pay attention to any contrastive or additive words, as they often signal the relationship between the sentence parts and guide you in selecting the correct answers.

## 3. Use Elimination Strategies

Eliminate answer choices that do not fit grammatically, stylistically, or logically. Even if you are not sure of the correct answer, narrowing down the choices can significantly increase your chances of guessing correctly.

## 4. Cross-Check Each Choice

Insert each potential answer into the blank and read the sentence to see if it makes sense both in the context of the sentence and the overall passage. This step is crucial for ensuring that the word or phrase fits perfectly.

### Practice Question Example

Consider the following practice question to understand how to apply these strategies:

### Prompt

Despite the _____ nature of the topic, the lecturer managed to explain the complex theories in terms that were easy to comprehend.

### Choices for the blank

- A) esoteric
- B) redundant
- C) simplistic
- D) erroneous
- E) accessible

### Analysis

First, understand the sentence structure and meaning. The key phrase here is "theories in terms that were easy to comprehend," which suggests that the topic might be difficult or obscure, yet was explained in an understandable way. Therefore, look for a word that implies complexity or difficulty.

- A) esoteric—fits because it means something that is understood by a small number of people with specialized knowledge or interest.

B) redundant—does not fit, as it suggests unnecessary repetition.
C) simplistic—does not fit; this would contradict the part of the sentence that implies the theories are complex.
D) erroneous—does not fit; this would imply the theories are incorrect.
E) accessible—does not fit; it contradicts the idea that the topic is challenging but was made easy to understand.

**Correct Answer**

A) esoteric

**Reviewing Your Answers**

After completing each practice question:

- Review why the correct answers are right and why the incorrect ones are wrong.
- Understand the nuances of each word choice and how they fit or do not fit in the context.
- Reflect on any mistakes to avoid similar errors in the future.

Practicing with Text Completion questions allows you to refine your ability to understand and interpret complex texts, enhance your vocabulary, and develop strategic test-taking skills. By incorporating a variety of practice questions into your study routine and analyzing them critically, you can significantly improve your performance on this challenging section of the GRE.

# Sentence Equivalence Strategies

Sentence Equivalence questions on the GRE Verbal Reasoning section test your ability to complete sentences in a manner that is coherent and contextually appropriate while ensuring the completed sentence maintains a consistent meaning, regardless of which of two possible answers is selected. Each question requires you to choose two answers from six options that, when inserted into the sentence, yield similar meanings. Mastering this question type involves a combination of vocabulary skills, reading comprehension, and critical reasoning. Here's how to approach Sentence Equivalence questions strategically.

**Develop Strong Vocabulary Skills**

*1. Contextual Vocabulary Learning*

Rather than merely memorizing word lists, focus on learning vocabulary in context. This approach helps you understand how words can change meaning based on their usage, which is crucial for tackling Sentence Equivalence questions where nuances matter significantly.

*2. Use Vocabulary Building Tools*

Leverage tools like flashcards, apps, and vocabulary books tailored for the GRE. Regularly engage with new words and review them periodically to enhance retention and recall.

## Analyze the Sentence Carefully

### 1. Understand the Sentence Structure

Before looking at the answer choices, read the sentence to grasp its structure and flow. Identify clues about the sentence's meaning or the relationships between different parts of the sentence.

### 2. Predict Possible Words

Try to fill in the blank with a word or words that seem appropriate based on your understanding of the sentence before looking at the given options. This method helps you anticipate the type of word needed without being biased by the answer choices.

## Evaluate Each Word Individually

### 1. Insert Each Word

Systematically evaluate each option by inserting it into the blank and determining if it makes sense both syntactically and semantically. This step helps in filtering out choices that do not fit.

### 2. Consider Connotations and Subtleties

Pay attention to the connotations of words—not just their direct meanings but also the feelings or ideas they may imply. This sensitivity can be crucial, especially when the sentence context calls for a specific tone or implication.

## Look for Synonymous Pairs

### 1. Identify Logical Pairs

After individually assessing each word, look for pairs among the remaining options. Effective pairs will convey a similar overall meaning to the sentence.

### 2. Double-Check for Consistency

Insert each word of your identified pairs into the sentence to ensure they both fit well and maintain the sentence's meaning. If one word seems slightly off in terms of tone or context, reconsider your choice.

## Practice Critical Reasoning

### 1. Rule Out Extreme Options

GRE often includes overly strong or absolute terms as trap answers. Be wary of words that seem extreme unless the sentence context specifically supports such a tone.

### 2. Be Skeptical of Surface-Level Similarities

Some words may appear similar or related but carry different meanings or connotations. Scrutinize choices closely, especially synonyms that might differ subtly in their typical usage.

### Regular Practice and Review

### 1. Practice with Authentic Resources

Use official practice questions and tests to familiarize yourself with the format and level of difficulty of Sentence Equivalence questions. GRE prep books and online resources can also offer quality practice questions.

### 2. Analyze Your Mistakes

Each practice session should end with a review of your answers, focusing particularly on any errors. Understanding why you chose incorrectly helps you refine your approach and avoid similar mistakes in the future.

Mastering Sentence Equivalence questions on the GRE requires more than just a good vocabulary—it demands analytical skills and precise judgment about word usage in context. By developing robust vocabulary skills, practicing effective strategies, and engaging in thorough review and self-assessment, you can significantly improve your ability to tackle these questions accurately and boost your verbal reasoning score.

# Practice Questions

Sentence Equivalence questions are a unique aspect of the GRE Verbal Reasoning section, designed to test not only your vocabulary but also your ability to use context to determine subtle differences in meaning. Practicing with these types of questions is crucial for success, as it helps refine your skills in discerning nuances and employing effective strategies. Ensure that your practice questions cover a wide range of topics and employ a variety of complex vocabulary. This diversity helps prepare you for the unpredictability of the actual exam conditions. Here's how to get the most out of Sentence Equivalence practice questions.

### Techniques for Effective Practice

### 1. Comprehensive Reading

Read the sentence thoroughly before looking at the answer choices. Try to understand the overall meaning and the role of the blank within the sentence. Predict what kind of word or words could fill the blank appropriately based on the context provided.

### 2. Evaluate Each Choice

After making an initial prediction, review each option independently. Insert each word into the blank and consider if it maintains the logical and stylistic integrity of the sentence. This process helps in narrowing down potential answers.

### 3. Look for Synonymous Relationships

Since you need to select two words that give the sentence a similar meaning, identify pairs among the choices that are synonymous or nearly synonymous in the context of the sentence. This step is crucial and often requires a deep understanding of word meanings and connotations.

### 4. Use Elimination

Cross out words that clearly do not fit either due to meaning or grammatical structure. Elimination can simplify decision-making, especially when choices are closely related or when the context is complex.

## Example Practice Question and Analysis

## Sentence

The author's argument, though _____, was convincing to those who frequently engage with the nuanced subject matter.

## Choices

- A) abstruse
- B) obvious
- C) clear
- D) recondite
- E) transparent
- F) evident

## Analysis

1. **Understand the context:** The sentence suggests that the argument is complex ("nuanced subject matter") but convincing.
2. **Predict a word:** Before looking at the choices, you might predict that the blank could be filled with a word meaning "complex" or "difficult to understand."

## Evaluate Each Choice

A) abstruse and D) recondite both mean obscure or hard to understand, fitting the context implied.

B) obvious, C) clear, E) transparent, and F) evident suggest clarity and simplicity, which contradict the hint provided by "nuanced subject matter."

## Select the Correct Answers

A) abstruse and D) recondite are the best fits as both maintain the sentence's meaning that the argument is complex yet persuasive.

## Reviewing Your Practice

After completing practice questions:

- **Review explanations:** Even if you got the answer right, review the explanation to understand why certain choices were correct and others were not.
- **Reflect on your reasoning:** Consider if your method of approaching the question was efficient and effective. Could your process improve?
- **Identify patterns:** Look for patterns in the types of errors you make, whether they're related to misunderstanding vocabulary or not picking up on contextual clues.

## Regular Practice and Feedback

Regular practice is essential for mastering Sentence Equivalence questions. It helps you familiarize yourself with the format, work on timing, and refine your approach to selecting the most fitting words. Additionally, getting feedback, whether through self-assessment or from a tutor, can provide insights into improving your strategies.

Effective practice with Sentence Equivalence questions enhances your ability to understand and manipulate language within the context provided. By systematically applying these strategies and regularly engaging with practice questions, you can improve both your vocabulary and your ability to discern subtleties in meaning, key skills for scoring well on the GRE Verbal Reasoning section.

# CHAPTER 4: Quantitative Reasoning

## Fundamentals of Math: Essential Concepts and Formulas

Success in the Quantitative Reasoning section of the GRE hinges on a solid foundation in fundamental mathematical concepts and formulas. This part of the test assesses your ability to understand, interpret, and analyze quantitative information using skills learned in high school mathematics courses up to the Algebra II level. Understanding these essential concepts and having a strong grasp of key formulas can significantly enhance your efficiency and accuracy on the test. Here's a comprehensive guide to the fundamental mathematical concepts and formulas you need to master for the GRE.

**Essential Mathematical Concepts**

*1. Arithmetic and Number Properties*

- Integers, fractions, and decimals
- Prime numbers, factors, and multiples
- Odd and even integers
- Arithmetic operations (addition, subtraction, multiplication, division)
- Exponents and roots
- Absolute values
- Percentage calculations
- Ratio and proportion

*2. Algebra*

- Solving linear equations and inequalities
- Solving quadratic equations (factoring, using the quadratic formula)
- Understanding and manipulating algebraic expressions
- Functions and their properties
- Systems of equations
- Inequalities involving absolute values

*3. Geometry*

- Properties of triangles (including special right triangles and Pythagorean theorem)

- Circle properties (radius, diameter, circumference, area)
- Polygon properties, including quadrilaterals
- Volume and surface area calculations for cubes, rectangular solids, cylinders, and spheres
- Coordinate geometry: lines, slopes, intercepts, distance, and midpoint formulas

## 4. Data Analysis

- Basic statistics (mean, median, mode, range, standard deviation)
- Interpretation of data sets
- Probability fundamentals
- Counting methods (permutations and combinations)

## Essential Formulas to Memorize

### 1. Arithmetic Formulas

- Percent change: (New Value – Old Value) / Old Value × 100%
- Simple interest: I = PRT (Interest = Principal × Rate × Time)

### 2. Algebra Formulas

- Quadratic formula: $x = [-b \pm \text{sqrt}(b^2-4ac)] / (2a)$
- Slope of a line: $(y_2 - y_1) / (x_2 - x_1)$
- Distance formula: $\text{sqrt}[(x_2 - x_1)^2 + (y_2 - y_1)^2]$

### 3. Geometry Formulas

- Area of a triangle: 0.5 × base × height
- Area of a rectangle: length × width
- Area of a circle: $\pi r^2$ (where r is the radius)
- Circumference of a circle: $2\pi r$
- Volume of a cylinder: $\pi r^2 h$ (where r is the radius and h is the height)

### 4. Data Analysis Formulas

- Probability: Number of favorable outcomes / Total number of outcomes
- Combination formula: $nCr = n! / [r!(n-r)!]$
- Permutation formula: $nPr = n! / (n-r)!$

## Tips for Utilizing Mathematical Concepts and Formulas

### 1. Practice Regularly

Regular practice using these concepts and formulas in the context of solving GRE-style questions is crucial. This not only helps in memorizing the formulas but also improves your ability to apply them effectively under timed conditions.

## 2. Create a Formula Sheet

Compile a cheat sheet with all essential formulas and review it regularly. This helps in reinforcing memory and provides a quick reference during practice sessions.

## 3. Focus on Application

Understanding a formula is one thing, but knowing when and how to apply it is critical. Work on applying formulas in various contexts to deepen your understanding and flexibility in problem solving.

## 4. Work on Weak Areas

Identify areas where you are less confident and focus your study efforts on these topics. Use practice problems to test your understanding and adjust your study plan accordingly.

# Tactics of Quantitative Comparisons

Quantitative Comparison questions form a significant part of the GRE Quantitative Reasoning section. These questions require you to compare two quantities (Quantity A and Quantity B) and determine the relationship between them. Mastering the tactics for these questions is crucial, as they test not only your mathematical skills but also your ability to critically evaluate and compare information quickly and accurately. Here's how to approach these types of questions effectively.

**Understanding the Question Format**

Quantitative Comparison questions present two quantities and four answer choices:

**Choice A:** Quantity A is greater.

**Choice B:** Quantity B is greater.

**Choice C:** The two quantities are equal.

**Choice D:** The relationship cannot be determined from the information given.

Your task is to analyze the quantities and select the correct relationship based on the given information.

**Tactics for Solving Quantitative Comparison Questions**

## 1. Simplify the Quantities

Before making any comparisons, simplify the expressions for Quantity A and Quantity B as much as possible. This might involve performing algebraic operations, factoring, or substituting simple values to make the comparison clearer.

## 2. Estimate and Approximate

When exact calculations are complex or time-consuming, estimation can be a powerful tool. Round numbers to perform quick calculations that can give you a general idea of which quantity is larger, or if they might be equal.

## 3. Consider Special Cases

Especially when variables are involved, consider special or extreme cases. For instance, test small numbers, negative numbers, or zero. Different values might affect the relationship between the quantities in ways that are not immediately obvious.

## 4. Plug in Numbers

For quantities involving variables, a useful tactic is to plug in specific numbers to see how the relationship changes. Choose numbers that are easy to work with, such as 1, -1, 0, or 2. This method can quickly reveal which quantity is larger or if the relationship depends on the variable's value.

## 5. Use Geometric and Visual Representations

If the problem involves geometric figures, draw them out. Often, visualizing the problem can help clarify relationships between different parts of a geometry question, such as lengths, angles, and areas.

## 6. Focus on Relative Sizes, Not Exact Values

Quantitative Comparisons do not require you to solve for exact values; you only need to determine the relative size of Quantity A to Quantity B. Keep your calculations focused on comparison rather than calculation.

## 7. Watch Out for Traps

Common traps in these questions include overlooking negative values or zero, misunderstanding the implications of absolute values, and forgetting about non-integer numbers. Always double-check that your comparison holds true for all possible values within the constraints of the problem.

## Strategic Approaches to Answer Choices

## 1. Eliminate Obviously Incorrect Answers

Use your initial analysis to rule out any clearly incorrect relationships. If you can ascertain that one quantity is definitely not greater than the other, immediately eliminate that option.

## 2. Use Symmetry and Manipulation

If manipulating one quantity affects both quantities equally (e.g., multiplying both by a positive number), use these operations to simplify comparisons without changing the underlying relationship.

### 3. Decide or Defer

If after an initial analysis, you're still unsure, mark the question and move on. It's often beneficial to return to tricky questions after solving easier ones, as a fresh look might reveal something you missed.

### Practice Regularly

Regular practice with Quantitative Comparison questions is essential. Use practice questions to familiarize yourself with common types of quantitative comparisons and to refine your approach to these questions. Review explanations thoroughly to understand why certain answers are correct, and learn from any mistakes to improve your accuracy and speed.

Quantitative Comparison questions require a blend of mathematical skills, critical thinking, and strategic testing tactics. By understanding the question structure, applying effective problem-solving tactics, and practicing regularly, you can significantly enhance your ability to tackle these questions confidently and correctly on the GRE.

# Practice Questions

Quantitative Comparison questions on the GRE require not just a strong grasp of mathematics but also strategic thinking and practice. These questions, which ask you to compare two quantities and determine the relationship between them, are unique in that they often do not require an exact calculation but a relative comparison. Effective practice with these types of questions is crucial to mastering them for the GRE. Here's how to make the most out of Quantitative Comparisons practice questions.

### Understanding Quantitative Comparison Questions

Before diving into practice, ensure you fully understand what Quantitative Comparison questions entail:

Quantity A and Quantity B: You are presented with two quantities whose relationship you need to evaluate.

### Four Standard Answer Choices

A) Quantity A is greater.
B) Quantity B is greater.
C) The two quantities are equal.
D) The relationship cannot be determined from the information given.

Your task is to determine the correct relationship based on mathematical operations or logical reasoning.

## Selecting High-Quality Practice Questions

### 1. Use Authentic Materials

To ensure you are practicing with questions that reflect the actual GRE format and difficulty level, use materials from reputable sources, particularly those from ETS, the makers of the GRE. Authentic practice questions will help you develop an accurate sense of the test's demands.

### 2. Variety and Difficulty

Include a variety of questions in your practice to cover all potential types of quantitative comparisons you might encounter. Make sure to practice with questions of varying difficulty to prepare for the range of questions on the actual test.

## Effective Techniques for Practicing

### 1. Simulate Test Conditions

When practicing, try to mimic test conditions. Time yourself and practice in a quiet environment. This will help you manage time pressure and build test-taking stamina, both crucial for success on test day.

### 2. Analyze Each Question

For each practice question, thoroughly analyze the given information. Simplify expressions if possible, and consider substituting specific values to see how they affect each quantity. This can provide insight into whether one quantity is consistently greater than the other, or if the relationship depends on variable values.

### 3. Focus on Strategy

Develop a consistent strategy for approaching these questions. Start by simplifying and rearranging the expressions to make comparison easier. Look for opportunities to cross-multiply, factor, or cancel terms. Always consider the implications of zero, negative values, and extreme cases.

### 4. Review Explanations

After completing each question, review the explanation carefully, even for questions you answered correctly. Understanding the reasoning behind the correct answer is as important as getting the question right. This review process will help you refine your strategies and avoid common pitfalls.

## Practice Question Example

## Compare Quantity A and Quantity B

**Quantity A:** The product of X and Y, where X= 3 and Y= -2

**Quantity B:** The product of X and Y, where X= -3 and Y= 2

**Choices**

A) Quantity A is greater.
B) Quantity B is greater.
C) The two quantities are equal.
D) The relationship cannot be determined from the information given.

**Correct Answer**

B) The two quantities are equal.

**Explanation**

For Quantity A, $X \times Y = 3 \times -2 = -6$

For Quantity B, $X \times Y = -3 \times 2 = -6$

Since both products equal -6, the correct answer is C.

**Utilizing Feedback and Adjusting Strategies**

After reviewing each question, take note of any errors or misconceptions. Adjust your approach based on this feedback. If you notice a pattern of mistakes related to a specific type of manipulation or a particular mathematical concept, focus your study on those areas.

Regular and strategic practice with Quantitative Comparison questions will enhance your ability to quickly and accurately determine relationships between quantities. This practice, combined with a thorough review of strategies and explanations, will prepare you well for tackling this challenging question type on the GRE.

# Problem-Solving Strategies

Problem-solving questions in the GRE Quantitative Reasoning section test your ability to use mathematical concepts to solve various types of numerical challenges. These questions can involve basic arithmetic, algebra, geometry, and data analysis. To excel in these questions, it's crucial to develop a robust set of problem-solving strategies that allow you to approach and solve these questions efficiently and accurately. Here's how you can enhance your problem-solving skills for the GRE.

**Understand the Problem**

*1. Read Carefully*

The first step in solving any problem is to understand what is being asked. Read the question carefully to determine exactly what is required. Pay attention to specific details and keywords that indicate the operations or concepts involved.

### 2. Identify the Information Provided

Take note of all the information provided in the question. Determine which pieces of information are relevant to solving the problem and which are distractors. This helps in focusing your calculations and reasoning on what truly matters.

### 3. Visualize the Problem

For geometry questions or problems involving spatial relationships, drawing a diagram can be immensely helpful. For algebraic problems, organizing information into equations or expressions can clarify the steps needed for a solution.

## Develop a Plan

### 1. Choose an Appropriate Method

Decide on the best method to solve the problem based on the information and your understanding of the question. This might involve algebraic manipulation, constructing a geometric diagram, or setting up a system of equations.

### 2. Break Down Complex Problems

If a problem seems complex, break it down into smaller, manageable parts. Solve each part step by step before combining the results to reach the final answer.

### 3. Use Logical Reasoning

Sometimes, particularly with quantitative comparison questions, logical reasoning can lead to a quicker solution than straightforward computation. Evaluate the relationships and patterns within the data to make logical deductions.

## Execute the Solution

### 1. Perform Calculations Carefully

Carry out your calculations with precision. A small error in calculation can lead to a wrong answer. Double-check figures, especially in complex calculations involving multiple steps.

### 2. Keep Track of Units

Pay close attention to units of measurement in problems involving physical quantities. Convert all units to the same system if necessary to avoid errors in calculation.

### 3. Simplify Your Answers

Ensure that your final answer is simplified as required by the question. This includes reducing fractions, simplifying square roots, or rounding to the required number of decimal places.

**Check and Reflect**

*1. Verify Your Answer*

After solving the problem, take a moment to verify if your answer makes sense in the context of the question. Check if the magnitude and direction of your answer align with what is logically expected.

*2. Use Alternative Methods*

If time permits, try to solve the problem using a different method as a cross-check. This could involve substituting your answer back into the problem or using an estimation technique to verify the accuracy of your solution.

*3. Review Mistakes*

If you find an error upon reviewing, analyze where it occurred. Understanding your mistakes is crucial for avoiding them in the future and for learning how to approach similar problems correctly.

**Continuous Practice and Adaptation**

*1. Practice Regularly*

Frequent practice with a variety of problem types is essential. Use practice tests and problems from reputable GRE prep materials to familiarize yourself with the range of potential problem-solving questions.

*2. Adapt Strategies*

As you practice, you may find certain strategies work better for you than others. Adapt your approach based on what increases your accuracy and efficiency. Personalize your problem-solving strategies to fit your strengths and weaknesses.

Mastering problem-solving for the GRE involves a combination of understanding problems, developing strategic plans, executing solutions carefully, and reflecting on your process. By employing these strategies and practicing regularly, you can significantly improve your performance in the Quantitative Reasoning section, enhancing both your speed and accuracy.

# Practice Problems

Problem-solving is a critical component of the GRE Quantitative Reasoning section, testing a wide range of mathematical skills from arithmetic to algebra and geometry. To excel in this area, engaging regularly with practice problems is essential. This not only helps in reinforcing mathematical concepts but also sharpens your analytical and time management skills. Here's a guide on how to effectively utilize practice problems to improve your problem-solving abilities for the GRE.

## Selecting the Right Practice Problems

### 1. Diverse Topics

Ensure your practice covers all mathematical topics that the GRE might test. This includes, but is not limited to, arithmetic, algebra, geometry, data analysis, and word problems. Using a variety of problems helps prepare you for the breadth of questions on the actual test.

### 2. Varying Difficulty Levels

Include problems of different difficulty levels in your practice sessions. Start with simpler problems to build confidence and understanding, then gradually move to more complex ones. This stepwise progression helps in building a solid foundation and tackling tougher questions effectively.

## Effective Strategies for Practice

### 1. Understand the Problem

Start each problem by carefully reading and understanding the question. Identify exactly what is being asked and note any given data or conditions. This initial comprehension is crucial to solving the problem correctly.

### 2. Plan Your Approach

Before jumping into calculations, plan your approach. Decide which mathematical principles and formulas are applicable and think about the steps you will take to reach the solution. Planning helps in solving the problem systematically and efficiently.

### 3. Execute with Accuracy

Carry out your planned solution methodically. Perform calculations carefully to avoid simple arithmetic errors, which are common under exam conditions. Ensure every step is logically sound and contributes to solving the problem.

### 4. Review Your Work

After solving each problem, review your solution to ensure it makes sense and addresses the question posed. Check your calculations and logical steps. If your answer does not seem right, revisit your approach and identify any errors or oversights.

## Tips for Working Through Practice Problems

### 1. Time Yourself

Practice under timed conditions to get used to the pacing of the GRE. This helps in developing time management skills that are crucial during the actual test. Gradually, you will learn how much time to allocate to each type of problem.

### 2. Use Scratch Paper Effectively

During practice, simulate test conditions by using scratch paper for calculations and sketches, just as you would in the actual GRE. Organize your work so that you can easily follow your thought process, which is helpful for reviewing solutions later.

### 3. Focus on Weak Areas

Identify areas where you struggle and focus more practice on those topics. Solving problems that challenge you improves your overall mathematical ability and confidence in handling similar questions during the test.

### 4. Learn from Mistakes

Analyzing why you got a problem wrong is as important as practicing. Understand what went wrong, whether it was a calculation error, a misunderstanding of the problem, or a misapplication of a mathematical concept. Learning from these mistakes is crucial for improvement.

**Practice Problem Example and Solution**

**Problem**

If $5x + 3 = 2x + 18$, what is the value of x?

**Solution**

Start by isolating x on one side of the equation:

$5x + 3 = 2x + 18$

$5x - 2x = 18 - 3$

$3x = 15$

$x = 5$

**Verification**

Plug $x = 5$ back into the original equation to check:

$5(5) + 3 = 2(5) + 18$

$25 + 3 = 10 + 18$

28 = 28 (True, hence x=5 is correct.)

Regular practice with a wide variety of problems is key to mastering the problem-solving component of the GRE. By incorporating these strategies into your study routine, you'll not only improve your mathematical skills but also your ability to think critically and work efficiently under pressure, greatly enhancing your performance on the GRE.

# Data Interpretation: Graphs and Charts

Data interpretation is a critical aspect of the GRE Quantitative Reasoning section, requiring test-takers to analyze and interpret information presented in various graphical formats. This skill tests your ability to extract and manipulate data to make logical conclusions, often under time constraints. Effective interpretation of graphs and charts is essential for answering questions accurately and efficiently. Here's a detailed guide on how to approach data interpretation in the GRE.

**Understanding Graphs and Charts**

The GRE can include several types of graphical representations:

- **Line graphs:** Show trends over time.
- **Bar charts:** Compare quantities in different categories.
- **Pie charts:** Represent proportions or percentages within a whole.
- **Scatter plots:** Indicate the relationship between two variables.
- **Tables:** Provide data in rows and columns for direct analysis.

Each type of graph or chart has specific features and common uses, which you should be able to identify and understand.

**Essential Skills for Interpreting Data**

*1. Identify Key Information*

Begin by identifying the most important elements of the graph or chart. Note the titles, labels, units of measurement, and scales. Understanding what each axis represents or what each segment of a pie chart denotes is crucial for accurate interpretation.

*2. Analyze Trends and Patterns*

Look for trends (increasing, decreasing), patterns (cyclical, seasonal), or outliers in data. For line graphs, observe how the data points are connected and what that suggests about changes over time. In bar charts, compare the heights or lengths of bars to gauge relative quantities.

*3. Interpret Relationships*

In scatter plots, determine the type of correlation between variables. Whether the relationship is positive, negative, or nonexistent will guide your interpretation and prediction based on the data presented.

### 4. Use Proportional Thinking

For pie charts, it's essential to think in terms of pie slices relative to the whole. Understand that each slice represents a fraction or percentage of the total, and use this to compare different sections directly.

## Strategies for Effective Data Interpretation

### 1. Cross-Reference Multiple Sources

Sometimes, you may need to integrate data from more than one graph or chart to answer a question. Cross-referencing ensures a comprehensive understanding of the data provided and can uncover insights that are not immediately obvious from one source alone.

### 2. Estimate and Approximate

Not all questions will require exact answers. Often, estimation or approximation is sufficient and can save time. Develop the skill to estimate values by sight, particularly when dealing with bar charts or line graphs

### 3. Focus on What's Asked

Direct your analysis based on the specific question asked. Avoid spending too much time analyzing interesting data that is irrelevant to the question. Always bring your focus back to what you need to find out.

### 4. Practice with Variety

Expose yourself to a wide range of graphs and charts during your preparation. Practice with different data sets and question types to build flexibility and familiarity with interpreting various data formats.

## Common Pitfalls to Avoid

### 1. Overlooking Key Details

Missing a crucial piece of information like a unit change or a break in the axis can lead to incorrect interpretations. Always review the graphs or charts carefully.

### 2. Misreading Data

Ensure you read the correct values from the graphs. For instance, misinterpreting the scale on an axis can significantly alter the data's meaning.

### 3. Ignoring Small Differences

In close comparisons, small differences can be critical. Pay attention to these details, as they could determine the correct answer.

Mastering data interpretation requires practice, attention to detail, and a systematic approach to analyzing graphical information. By developing these skills, you enhance your ability to quickly and accurately process quantitative information, a key asset for achieving a high score on the GRE Quantitative Reasoning section. Regular engagement with practice problems and a focus on strategy will equip you to tackle data interpretation questions with confidence.

# Practice Sets

Data interpretation is an integral component of the GRE Quantitative Reasoning section, testing your ability to analyze and make decisions based on graphical data. To excel in this section, it's essential to practice with sets that mimic the complexity and variety of charts, graphs, and tables you will encounter on the actual exam. Here's a comprehensive guide on how to effectively use data interpretation practice sets to enhance your skills.

**Choosing the Right Practice Sets**

### 1. Variety in Graphical Representations

Ensure your practice sets include a wide range of graphical representations such as line graphs, bar charts, pie charts, scatter plots, and tables. Each type requires specific interpretation skills and the ability to cross-reference data among multiple sources.

### 2. Realistic Data Sets

Select practice sets that offer realistic data scenarios you might encounter in academic or professional settings. This prepares you for the types of questions on the GRE and helps develop your ability to interpret real-world data.

### 3. Graduated Difficulty

Start with simpler data sets to build your foundational skills and gradually progress to more complex ones. This method helps you develop confidence and competence without becoming overwhelmed.

**Effective Strategies for Using Practice Sets**

### 1. Simulate Exam Conditions

Practice under conditions that simulate the actual test to accustom yourself to the pressure and time constraints of the GRE. Use a timer to ensure you are not only getting the questions right but also working efficiently.

## 2. Analyze Each Graph Carefully

For each practice problem, start by thoroughly analyzing the graph or chart. Note what each axis represents, understand the units of measurement, and identify any trends, patterns, or outliers in the data. Recognizing these elements is crucial for answering questions accurately.

## 3. Practice Cross-Referencing

Many GRE data interpretation questions require information from multiple graphs or charts to be synthesized. Practice combining data from different sources to answer more complex questions. This skill is crucial for the multi-source reasoning questions you might face on the test.

## 4. Focus on What's Relevant

Sharpen your ability to quickly identify the most relevant pieces of information needed to answer the question. Avoid getting bogged down in interesting but irrelevant data, which can waste time and divert your focus from the main objective.

## Review and Reflect

## 1. Check Your Answers Thoroughly

After completing each set, carefully check your answers against the solutions. Pay attention not only to whether you got the question right but also to why the correct answers are what they are. Understand any errors in your interpretation or calculation.

## 2. Reflect on Your Process

Reflect on how you approached each problem. Were there ways you could have been more efficient? Did you miss any crucial data because you skimmed too quickly? Reflection helps improve both your speed and accuracy.

## 3. Develop a Checklist

Based on common mistakes or oversights, develop a personal checklist to use when interpreting data. This might include steps like double-checking axes labels and units, confirming trends, or ensuring all parts of the question have been answered.

## Advanced Tips for Mastery

## 1. Practice with Non-GRE Materials

To broaden your experience, practice interpreting data from sources outside of GRE prep materials, such as academic journals, business reports, or economic reviews. This exposure to a wider range of data presentation styles can enhance your adaptability and analytical skills.

## 2. Teach What You Learn

One effective way to deepen your understanding is to explain how you solved a data interpretation problem to someone else. Teaching forces you to clarify your thoughts and solidify your grasp of the material.

Regular practice with a diverse set of realistic data interpretation questions is essential for mastering this section of the GRE. By following these strategies, you will not only improve your ability to work with graphical data but also enhance your overall test-taking strategy, ensuring that you are well-prepared for any data interpretation challenges on exam day.

# CHAPTER 5: Practice Tests

## Section-specific: Overview and Instructions of Analytical Writing

Welcome to the Analytical Writing section of your GRE practice tests. This section is designed to evaluate your ability to think critically and to communicate your ideas in writing. The "Analyze an Issue" task assesses your ability to think critically about a topic of general interest and to express your thoughts about it in writing. Each essay topic poses a complex issue to which there are no absolute "correct" responses. Here are detailed instructions and an overview to guide you through this practice test.

**Overview**

**Task**: Analyze an Issue

**Time Allotted**: 30 minutes

**Objective**: To assess your ability to develop an argument about a given topic using reasoning and supporting evidence, and to communicate your thoughts in a clear and coherent manner.

**Instructions for the "Analyze an Issue" Task**

**Understanding the Issue:** At the beginning of the test, you will be presented with a brief statement on a topic. This topic will be of general interest and will not require any specific knowledge. The issue will have multiple perspectives; there is no "right" or "wrong" stance.

**Developing Your Position:** You must choose a position on the issue—either agree or disagree with the statement—and develop your response by using logical reasoning, examples, and evidence. It's important to articulate your position clearly and demonstrate how your reasoning supports your viewpoint.

**Writing the Essay**

**Introduction:** Start with an introduction that states your position on the issue and previews the points you will use to support your position.

**Body paragraphs:** Each paragraph should discuss a single compelling reason for your position. Provide specific examples and evidence to support your arguments. Ensure each paragraph logically transitions to the next.

**Conclusion:** Conclude with a paragraph that summarizes your key points and reinforces your position on the issue.

**Time management:** Allocate your time wisely—spend a few minutes planning your essay, most of your time writing it, and a few minutes at the end revising it to correct any glaring errors and refine your arguments.

**What to Focus On**

**Clarity and precision:** Be clear and precise in your writing. Avoid vague language and unsupported generalizations.

**Logical structure:** Organize your essay logically. Your arguments should flow naturally from one to the next.

**Examples and evidence:** Use relevant examples and evidence to back up your claims. Real-world examples, hypothetical situations, and personal experiences are all valid.

**Language and grammar:** Pay attention to your language and grammar. While a few minor errors won't necessarily disqualify your essay, clear and grammatical writing can only help your score.

**Scoring Criteria**

Your essay will be scored on a scale of 0 to 6, based on the clarity and logic of the arguments presented, the relevance and support of examples used, the organization of the essay, and the competency of the writing.

By completing this practice test, you'll gain insight into how well you can develop and articulate your thoughts under timed conditions. Use this exercise as an opportunity to refine your analytical writing skills and to improve your ability to formulate compelling arguments.

# Practice Test 1: Analyze an Issue

In this section of the Analytical Writing portion of your GRE practice, you will engage directly with a prompt designed to challenge your reasoning and persuasive writing skills. The "Analyze an Issue" task mirrors the structure and intellectual challenge presented by the actual GRE and is crafted to evaluate your ability to construct a coherent argument under time constraints.

**Test Section: Analyze an Issue**

**Prompt**

"In an age where quick decisions often bring success, individuals who spend a great deal of time deliberating over issues are likely to find themselves overshadowed by those who act more quickly."

## Task Instructions

You are required to analyze the issue presented in the prompt and construct a clear and compelling argument for your position on the issue. Here's how you can effectively approach this task:

## Read the Issue Carefully

Understand every aspect of the statement. Note any assumptions, implications, or possible misconceptions within the issue.

## Choose Your Position

Decide whether you agree or disagree with the statement. Your position does not need to be black or white; you could argue that the statement is only sometimes true depending on certain conditions.

## Writing Your Essay

- Introduction
- Body paragraphs
- Conclusion

## Review and Revise

If time allows, re-read your essay to make corrections. Look for any grammatical errors, awkward phrasing, or points that could be clearer or more persuasive.

Ensure that the conclusion effectively encapsulates and reinforces your argument.

## Completion

Upon completion, your essay should present a well-rounded argument that demonstrates your ability to dissect and discuss complex issues critically. It should reflect both your depth of understanding of the topic and your capacity to communicate effectively through written words.

This task tests your analytical writing skills and your ability to formulate and support complex ideas under a strict time limit. It is an essential component of your GRE preparation, reflecting the type of cognitive and rhetorical challenge you will face on exam day.

# Answer Sheet

**Issue Prompt**

"In an age where quick decisions often bring success, individuals who spend a great deal of time deliberating over issues are likely to find themselves overshadowed by those who act more quickly."

**Answer Sheet for Analytical Writing: Analyze an Issue**

**Essay Structure**

*Introduction*

Thesis Statement: Clearly state whether you agree, disagree, or partially agree with the statement. Offer a brief rationale for your stance.
Example: "While rapid decision-making can indeed confer competitive advantages in certain scenarios, a nuanced approach that includes deliberate contemplation remains crucial for long-term success in many fields."

*Body Paragraphs*

Paragraph 1: Argument Supporting Your Thesis
Main Idea: Present a compelling reason that supports your viewpoint.
Evidence/Example: Provide examples where quick decisions are essential (e.g., emergency responses, stock market decisions).
Analysis: Explain how these examples support your thesis.
Paragraph 2: Counterargument and Rebuttal
Main Idea: Address a potential counterargument to acknowledge the complexity of the issue.
Counterargument Example: Admit that in fast-paced industries like technology or finance, quick decision-making can lead to significant advancements and opportunities.
Rebuttal Example: However, argue that strategic deliberation can prevent costly mistakes and provide more sustainable success.
Paragraph 3: Further Supporting Argument
Main Idea: Offer another perspective or example that supports your thesis.
Evidence/Example: Discuss fields where deliberation is essential (e.g., medical decisions, legal proceedings).
Analysis: Detail how thoughtful deliberation in these examples leads to better outcomes than hasty decisions.

*Conclusion*

Summary: Briefly recap the main arguments made in favor of your position.
Restatement of Thesis: Reinforce your thesis with the insights gained from the body paragraphs.
Closing Thought: Perhaps suggest a balanced approach that combines timely decision-making with thoughtful deliberation as a formula for success in various domains.

## Writing and Revision Tips

Clarity and Precision: Ensure your arguments are articulated clearly. Avoid ambiguous language.
Logical Flow: Maintain a logical progression of ideas. Use transitions effectively.
Support and Examples: Utilize specific examples to substantiate your points. Examples should be relevant and strengthen your arguments.
Grammar and Style: Pay attention to grammar, syntax, and style. Clear and error-free writing enhances the readability and impact of your essay.

## Scoring Criteria (For Self-Assessment)

Clarity and logic of arguments
Relevance and support for examples used
Organization and structure of the essay
Command of written English

This structured guide serves as a practical tool for planning, composing, and revising your essay response to the given Issue Prompt. It is designed to help you articulate a well-reasoned argument and demonstrate effective written communication skills, crucial for achieving a high score on the GRE Analytical Writing section.

# Section-specific: Overview and Instructions of Verbal Reasoning

Welcome to the Verbal Reasoning section of your GRE practice tests. This component is designed to evaluate your ability to analyze written material, synthesize information from it, comprehend the meanings of words, sentences, and entire texts, and apply reasoning skills.

## Overview

**Content areas:** This section involves three types of questions: Reading Comprehension, Text Completion, and Sentence Equivalence.

**Objective:** To assess your ability to analyze written material, understand and interpret nuances, and reason logically from given data.

**Test format:** The section is divided into two parts: the first part consists of 12 questions with an 18-minute time allocation, and the second part consists of 15 questions with a 23-minute time allocation, making a total of 27 questions to be completed in 41 minutes.

**Instructions for the Verbal Reasoning Section**

### Reading Comprehension

**Tasks:** You will encounter passages of various lengths and complexities and will answer questions that test your understanding of their content, ranging from main ideas and details to the author's tone and assumed intentions.

**Strategy:** Approach each passage methodically, noting key points and relationships. Use marginal notes or mental summaries to keep track of content, especially for longer passages.

### Text Completion

**Tasks:** Fill in the blanks within single or multiple sentences to complete the text logically based on the provided options.

**Strategy:** Focus on the logic of the sentence. Identify clues within the sentence that hint at the correct answers and consider how each word option alters the meaning of the sentence.

### Sentence Equivalence

**Tasks:** Choose two answers that complete a sentence coherently and synonymously, demonstrating both a correct and consistent use of language.

**Strategy:** Look for keywords or phrases in the sentence that hint at the overall meaning and focus on selecting words that reflect this understanding in two different but equivalent ways.

### Timing and Pacing

**First section timing:** Spend about 1.5 minutes per question in the first part (12 questions in 18 minutes).

**Second section timing:** Allocate slightly over 1.5 minutes per question in the second part (15 questions in 23 minutes).

**General time management:** Manage your time by initially responding to questions you find straightforward and marking more challenging questions for review if time permits at the end.

### Additional Tips

- **Regular practice:** Engage regularly with practice questions to become familiar with the types and formats of questions.
- **Vocabulary building:** Enhance your ability to excel at Sentence Equivalence and Text Completion questions by improving your vocabulary through consistent practice and reading.
- **Reading for structure:** Develop your skills in reading comprehension by focusing on the structure and argumentative elements of complex academic texts.
- **Reflective review:** Always review your practice test answers to understand your mistakes and refine your strategies accordingly.

This structured approach will prepare you to tackle the Verbal Reasoning section effectively by understanding the detailed demands of the test, developing targeted strategies for different question types, and enhancing your overall reading and reasoning skills.

# Practice Test 2: Reading Comprehension

Here's a simulation of the Verbal Reasoning section of the GRE, divided into two parts to reflect the actual exam format. This includes a variety of Reading Comprehension, Text Completion, and Sentence Equivalence questions.

**Passage:**

When we study law, we are not studying a mystery but a well-known profession. We are studying what we shall want in order to appear before judges, or to advise people in such a way as to keep them out of court. The reason why it is a profession, why people will pay lawyers to argue for them or to advise them, is that in societies like ours the command of the public force is intrusted to the judges in certain cases, and the whole power of the state will be put forth, if necessary, to carry out their judgments and decrees. People want to know under what circumstances and how far they will run the risk of coming against what is so much stronger than themselves, and hence it becomes a business to find out when this danger is to be feared. The object of our study, then, is prediction, the prediction of the incidence of the public force through the instrumentality of the courts.

The means of the study are a body of reports, of treatises, and of statutes, in this country and in England, extending back for six hundred years, and now increasing annually by hundreds. In these sibylline leaves are gathered the scattered prophecies of the past upon the cases in which the axe will fall. These are what properly have been called the oracles of the law. Far the most important and pretty nearly the whole meaning of every new effort of legal thought is to make these prophecies more precise, and to generalize them into a thoroughly connected system. The process is one, from a lawyer's statement of a case, eliminating as it does all the dramatic elements with which his client's story has clothed it, and retaining only the facts of legal import, up to the final analyses and abstract universals of theoretic jurisprudence. The reason why a lawyer does not mention that his client wore a white hat when he made a contract, while Mrs. Quickly would be sure to dwell upon it along with the parcel gilt goblet and the sea-coal fire, is that he foresees that the public force will act in the same way whatever his client had upon his head. It is to make the prophecies easier to be remembered and to be understood that the teachings of the decisions of the past are put into general propositions and gathered into textbooks, or that statutes are passed in a general form. The primary rights and duties with which jurisprudence busies itself again are nothing but prophecies. One of the many evil effects of the confusion between legal and moral ideas, about which I shall have something to say in a moment, is that theory is apt to get the cart before the horse, and consider the right or the duty as something existing apart from and independent of the consequences of its breach, to which certain sanctions are added afterward. But, as I shall try to show, a legal duty so called is nothing but a prediction that if a man does or omits certain things he will be made to suffer in this or that way by judgment of the court; and so of a legal right.

The number of our predictions when generalized and reduced to a system is not unmanageably large. They present themselves as a finite body of dogma which may be mastered within a reasonable time. It is a great mistake to be frightened by the ever-increasing number of reports. The reports of a given jurisdiction in the course of a generation take up pretty much the whole body of the law, and restate it from the present point of view. We could reconstruct the corpus from them if all that went before were burned.

**Questions:**

1. Which of the following most closely resembles proper theoretic jurisprudence as it is described by the author?

    A. A philosopher starting with certain assumed truths and common sense principles, then combining them and teasing out their implications to deduce what must be done to resolve ethical dilemmas

    B. A philosopher conducting thought experiments to test the soundness of a theory under extreme cases, documenting where the theory produced counterintuitive or paradoxical results

    C. A biologist noticing trends in a set of collected data, accounting and controlling for extranious variables, and creating a general model that can be applied to other relevant instances

    D. An anthropologist conducting interviews and listening to the oral traditions of several different cultures, then constructing a theory that describes the development of cultural values in human societies

    E. A physicist working with mathematical models to construct a theory, then testing this theory by conducting experiments


2. With which of the following positions would the author of this passage most likely disagree?

    A. Legal principles are mainly aids to help guess how a law case will turn out.

    B. While one can never learn every fact of the law, such learning is unnecessary to mastering the law.

    C. In practicing law, one can only make predictions on how a particular case might turn out, and never certain ones.

    D. There is nothing irrelevant to the practice of law.

    E. While there may be a relationship between morality and law, the law is not simply a codification and enforcement of ethical principles.


3. Which of the following views is most nearly opposed to the main thesis of the author?

A.  The proper subject of the study of law itself, as opposed to individual laws, is to derrive and deduce legal principles from first principles.
B.  The law considers no detail irrelevant, no piece of evidence too small, in making its decisions; the most weighty matters are sometimes decided on what seem to be the most trivial of details.
C.  Nobody can escape the "long arm of the law," and all fear it; thus, they seek the advice of attornies and counselors to avoid crossing those well-defined lines that are poorly known to the layman in which the law must act.
D.  The law is often obscure, and open to interpretation; thus, the best lawyer is the one who can work in these "penumbras of the law," fashioning the best interpretation of it in the open spaces between certain cases.
E.  The past dictates the present, and what has come before what comes now—indeed, what is to come. Thus, the student of law who knows the greatest part of the body of past law will have the best chance of predicting the outcome of present and future cases.

4. Which of the following best captures the primary point of the final paragraph?

A.  New cases merely rehash and go over old issues in ways an experienced practicioner will have seen before. As such, one need not study old decisions and principles, as newer ones present them in exactly the same way.
B.  It is not necessary to learn every single court decision, statute, or legal determination that has been issued in the last 600 years, as the relevent issues are recapitulated and reinterpreted regularly.
C.  As laws are valid only in particular jurisdictions, and legal principles are derrived from these laws, it therefore follows that legal principles are valid only in certain jurisdictions; thus, while the body of law worldwide might seem overwhelming, one need only learn the laws of the jurisdictions in which one practices, and likewise only the principles that can be deduced from them.
D.  The body of law, in its statutes, principles, and decisions, is increasing at such a rate that anyone who would hope to master it must constantly "run to stay in place;" by the time a practicioner has digested some part of the legal corpus, new decisions and statutes have supplanted what was learned.
E.  The body of law is ever-increasing, with courts adding to it by the moment; as such, it is impossible to ever truly learn the whole of the law in the course of a single lifetime.

## Passage:

To present a general view of the Common Law, other tools are needed besides logic. It is something to show that the consistency of a system requires a particular result, but it is not all. The life of the law has not been logic: it has been experience. The felt necessities of the time, the prevalent moral and political theories, intuitions of public policy, avowed or unconscious, even the prejudices which judges share with their fellow-men, have had a good deal more to do than the syllogism in determining the rules by which men should be governed. The law embodies the story of a nation's development through many centuries, and it cannot be dealt with as if it contained only the axioms and corollaries of a book of mathematics. In order to know what it is, we must know what it has been, and what it tends to become. We must alternately consult history and existing theories of legislation. But the most difficult labor will be to understand the combination of the two into new products at every stage. The substance of the law at any given time pretty nearly corresponds, so far as it goes, with what is then understood to be convenient; but its form and machinery, and the degree to which it is able to work out desired results, depend very much upon its past.

In Massachusetts today, while, on the one hand, there are a great many rules which are quite sufficiently accounted for by their manifest good sense, on the other, there are some which can only be understood by reference to the infancy of procedure among the German tribes, or to the social condition of Rome under the Decemvirs.

I shall use the history of our law so far as it is necessary to explain a conception or to interpret a rule, but no further. In doing so there are two errors equally to be avoided both by writer and reader. One is that of supposing, because an idea seems very familiar and natural to us, that it has always been so. Many things which we take for granted have had to be laboriously fought out or thought out in past times. The other mistake is the opposite one of asking too much of history. We start with man full grown. It may be assumed that the earliest barbarian whose practices are to be considered, had a good many of the same feelings and passions as ourselves.

**Questions:**

5. Which of the following statements would the author of this passage be most likely to agree with?

    A. "Rights and responsibilities flow from past decisions and so count as legal, not just when they are explicit in these decisions but also when they follow from the principles of personal and political morality the explicit decisions presuppose by way of justification."
    B. "Justice is what the judge had for breakfast."
    C. "We must always stand by past decisions, and not disturb the undisturbed."
    D. "We must beware of the pitfall of antiquarianism, and must remember that for our purposes our only interest in the past is for the light it throws upon the present."
    E. "Law aims to lay principle over practice to show the best route to a better future, keeping the right faith with the past."

6. Which of the following statements would the author of the passage be most likely to disagree with most strongly?

    A. There is, strictly speaking, no law apart from society; what is found in the one is found in the other.
    B. The story of law is seen in its history, a history that includes the present day and even the future.

C. Human nature does not change, but the circumstances in which men live do; thus, some laws of great antiquity ought to still be followed, but others have outlived their use.
D. The law is itself lawful, and the one who understands its first principles can reason to its conclusions.
E. In studying the paths of the law, we can discern certain principles that appear time and again, and, inasmuch as they are useful for the present, ought to learn them.

7. Each of the following can be inferred from the passage EXCEPT _____.

    A. laws generally reflect the societies in which they were enacted
    B. there are some contemporary laws based in ancient Roman law
    C. there is no role for systematic logic in the interpretation of laws
    D. human nature has generally been the same throughout history
    E. many laws of ancient origin that have little relevance to contemporary society were once relevant to an older social order

8. Which of the following best describes the purpose of the underlined paragraph in the passage?

    A. A specific example used as evidence to bolster a premise in an earlier argument
    B. A set of examples used to illustrate an assertion earlier in the passage
    C. An example illustrating the effects of applying procedures advocated for earlier
    D. A rhetorical contrast between good sense and adherance to ancient tradition
    E. A contrast between two approaches to understanding a single body of law

**Passage:**

The first thought that men had concerning the heavenly bodies was an obvious one: they were lights. There was a greater light to rule the day, a lesser light to rule the night, and there were the stars also.

In those days there seemed an immense difference between the earth upon which men stood and the bright objects that shone down upon it from the heavens above. The earth seemed to be vast, dark, and motionless; the celestial lights seemed to be small, and moved and shone. The earth was then regarded as the fixed center of the universe, but the Copernican theory has since deprived it of this pride of place. Yet from another point of view, the new conception of its position involves a promotion, since the earth itself is now regarded as a heavenly body of the same order as some of those that shine down upon us. It is amongst them, and it too moves and shines—shines, as some of them do, by reflecting the light of the sun. Could we transport ourselves to a neighboring world, the earth would seem a star, not distinguishable in kind from the rest.

But as men realized this, they began to ask, "Since this world from a distant standpoint must appear as a star, would not a star, if we could get near enough to it, show itself also as a world? This world teems with life; above all, it is the home of human life. Men and women, gifted with feeling, intelligence, and character, look upward from its surface and watch the shining members of the heavenly host. Are none of these the home of beings gifted with like powers, who watch in their turn the movements of that shining point that is our world?"

This is the meaning of the controversy on the Plurality of Worlds which excited so much interest some sixty years ago, and has been with us more or less ever since. It is the desire to recognize the presence in the orbs around us of beings like ourselves, possessed of personality and intelligence, lodged in an organic body.

This is what is meant when we speak of a world being "inhabited." It would not, for example, at all content us if we could ascertain that Jupiter was covered by a shoreless ocean, rich in every variety of fish, or that the hard rocks of the Moon were delicately veiled by lichens. Just as no richness of vegetation and no fullness and complexity of animal life would justify an explorer in describing some land that he had discovered as being "inhabited" if no men were there, so we cannot rightly speak of any other world as being "inhabited" if it is not the home of intelligent life.

On the other hand, of necessity we are precluded from extending our inquiry to the case of disembodied intelligences, if such be conceived possible. All created existences must be conditioned, but if we have no knowledge of what those conditions may be, or means for attaining such knowledge, we cannot discuss them. Nothing can be affirmed, nothing denied, concerning the possibility of intelligences existing on the Moon or even in the Sun if we are unable to ascertain under what limitations those particular intelligences subsist.

The only beings, then, the presence of which would justify us in regarding another world as "inhabited" are such as would justify us in applying that term to a part of our own world. They must possess intelligence and consciousness on the one hand; on the other, they must likewise have corporeal form. True, the form might be imagined as different from that we possess, but, as with ourselves, the intelligent spirit must be lodged in and expressed by a living material body. <u>Our inquiry is thus rendered a physical one; it is the necessities of the living body that must guide us in it; a world unsuited for living organisms is not, in the sense of this enquiry, a "habitable" world.</u>

**Questions:**

9. Which of the following statements does the passage most strongly suggest that the author would agree with?

    A. Science could possibly discover the truth about anything that could possibly exist.
    B. The work of Copernicus was a necessary step for people to be able to think of other worlds as possibly inhabited.
    C. There are some worlds that are home to beings without bodies, even though we cannot study these beings.
    D. The controversy of the plurality of worlds is settled.
    E. Every star is a world like our own.

10. Which of the following CANNOT be inferred from the passage?

    A. No uninhabited world is the home of intelligent beings.
    B. Some uninhabited world could be the home of intelligent beings.
    C. Some inhabited world could be the home of non-intelligent beings.
    D. Some uninhabited world could be the home of non-intelligent beings.
    E. Every inhabited world is the home of intelligent beings.


11. Which of the following best describes the primary purpose of the underlined final sentence of the passage?

    A. A key assumption assumed by earlier arguments that, if true, would validate them
    B. An additional, secondary conclusion that can be derived from the primary conclusion of the passage
    C. The primary conclusion of the passage, supported by an earlier subordinate conclusion
    D. A question raised by the conclusion of the passage that will be investigated later
    E. An empirical observation that must guide the theoretical model under consideration


12. Which of the following best describes the tone of the first three paragraphs?

    A. Witty and ironic
    B. Objective and serious
    C. Formal and didactic
    D. Reflective and philosophical
    E. Elegiac and wistful


13. Which of the following most accurately describes the main idea of the passage?

    A. In order for a world to be considered inhabited, it must have intelligent life with material bodies.
    B. The inhabitants of other worlds could have very different bodies than those of humans.
    C. As science has progressed, people have wondered if there are other worlds that might be inhabited by creatures like ourselves.
    D. Advances in science have allowed us to contemplate whether other worlds are inhabited.
    E. The presence of non-intelligent life, like lichens or oysters, is not sufficient to make another world inhabited.


14. Which of the following best describes the structure of the passage?

    A. Giving the history of the development of a theory; mentioning a consequence of this development; describing necessary conditions for a state of affairs; drawing conclusions from these conditions

B. Describing a scientific problem; laying out some possible solutions to that problem; describing a new theory that addresses some of the common problems in previous models; addressing the limits of how this new theory can be applied

C. Explaining the history of a scientific discipline; making deductions from the progress of this discipline; describing sufficient conditions for further progress in a particular area; laying out avenues for future investigation

D. Describing the results of empirical investigations; conducting a thought experiment based on these results; describing further observations that fit both the initial investigation and the thought experiment; creating a new theoretical model

E. Describing the development of a theoretical model; explaining how this model influenced more recent observations; describing a new application for the kinds of observations influenced by this model; mentioning how a different model could also account for these observations

15. What is the primary purpose of the fourth paragraph?

A. To introduce a premise that will be used to support a conclusion in the final paragraph

B. To transition between the historical and metaphysical survey of the opening paragraphs and the logical arguments of the following ones

C. To provide an introduction and historical context for the controversy of the plurality of worlds

D. To reach a secondary conclusion important to the main argument of the overall passage

E. To present evidence that will be used to counter an opposing argument

# Answer Sheet

1. **Correct Answer:** A biologist noticing trends in a set of collected data, accounting and controlling for extraneous variables, and creating a general model that can be applied to other relevant instances

**Explanation:** The form of theoretic jurisprudence, according to the author, is one that very closely resembles an empirical science-that is, it draws conclusions based on trends noted from relevant data, with extraneous or distracting factors accounted for or removed, used to create models that predict future results. As such, the most closely analogous case would be the one that follows this pattern, especially the necessary condition that the model be useful for predicting future cases.

2. **Correct Answer:** There is nothing irrelevant to the practice of law.

**Explanation:** The author states ("The reason why a lawyer does not mention that his client wore a white hat when he made a contract") that there are some details that are irrelevant in making legal arguments. Other responses can be supported by specific statements in the passage (e.g., "It is to make the prophecies easier to be remembered and to be understood that the teachings of the decisions of the past are put into general propositions and gathered into textbooks" and its surrounding context supporting the notion that legal principles are guides to helping predict the outcome of a case).

3. **Correct Answer:** The proper subject of the study of law itself, as opposed to individual laws, is to derive and deduce legal principles from first principles.

**Explanation:** While it is unlikely that the author would agree with any of the responses, as they either have no relevance to the passage or contradict details of it, the credited response is the one that most nearly contradicts the main idea of the passage: that jurisprudence is concerned not with deriving legal principles from eternal first principles of morality, but with predicting how courts will act in certain situations given past cases and statutes.

4. **Correct Answer:** It is not necessary to learn every single court decision, statute, or legal determination that has been issued in the last 600 years, as the relevent issues are recapitulated and reinterpreted regularly.

**Explanation:** The final paragraph claims that, while the already overwhelming body of law in its statutes and decisions is growing by the moment at a rate nobody could ever hope to keep up with, mastering every single detail of the centuries-old corpus is not necessary as the main issues are reinterpreted in ways relevent to contemporary society in every generation. The credited response most closely matches this point in its details, capturing not only the overwhelming size of the legal corpus and its inexorable increase, but also the nature of how it is recapitulated in every generation and the practical consequences for legal practice.

5. **Correct Answer:** "We must beware of the pitfall of antiquarianism, and must remember that for our purposes our only interest in the past is for the light it throws upon the present."

**Explanation:** The author's attitude towards past legal decisions and statutes is one in which this history has its uses for understanding the present, but there are certain limits to its use; as soon as a historical approach ceases to be useful in "explaining a conception or interpreting a rule," it is to be abandoned. Thus, while an understanding of legal history is useful to a degree, it is not to be used to the exclusion of other methods. The credited response is the one that best shows this limited approach to the use of legal history. While some other responses mention history, and, indeed, how present practice can flow from the past, they do not mention the limits that ought to be placed on deference to the past; indeed, the requirement in one response that legal reasoning "follow from the principles of personal and political morality" of past legislators contradicts Holmes's assertion that there are strict limits to the use of history.

6. **Correct Answer:** The law is itself lawful, and the one who understands its first principles can reason to its conclusions.

**Explanation:** The credited response most closely matches the idea, rejected by the author, that law can be conducted as if by syllogism, proceeding from known premises always and truly via logic to certain conclusions. The picture painted by the author is one in which many factors—history, ethics, society and its changes, and
"what is then considered to be convenient"-combine and meld to form the body of law, a sometimes disorderly and not strictly logical body. The other responses, while perhaps not always strictly in agreement with all of the author's nuances and ideas, do not so directly contradict the central thesis of the passage.


7. **Correct Answer:** there is no role for systematic logic in the interpretation of laws

**Explanation:** While the author does spend the first paragraph attacking the idea that law is a strictly logical discipline, he never says that it is not one in which logical procedures and operations are not to be used-just that their use must be subordinated to experience. Other responses can be validly extrapolated from specific citations in the text (e.g., "The felt necessities of the time ... should be governed" supporting the idea that laws reflect the societies in which they were enacted), while the idea that there is nothing formally logical in the practice of law cannot.


8. **Correct Answer:** A set of examples used to illustrate an assertion earlier in the passage

**Explanation:** The passage makes an allusion to a body of examples - the laws of Massachusetts - in order to show through an example how a certain assertion made in the previous paragraph - that law reflects what is convenient at a certain place and time and its present form reflects its past - might be justified; however, it cannot be called a specific example (no particular law of the Commonwealth is referred to, much less how that law is indebted to ancient Europe), nor one that bolsters a premise in an earlier argument. The paragraph does not illustrate procedures being applied, as no specific procedures are being discussed here; nor does it contrast two approaches to the study of any subject, but rather the reasons behind the form and functioning of laws; nor does it make a merely rhetorical contrast.


9. **Correct Answer:** The work of Copernicus was a necessary step for people to be able to think of other worlds as possibly inhabited.

**Explanation:** The author implies that the Copernican revolution was a necessary first step to people thinking of the Earth as one celestial body among many ("the new [Copernican] conception of [the Earth's] position involves a promotion, since the earth itself is now regarded as a heavenly body of the same order as some of those that shine down upon us"), which was itself a necessary step for people to also think of other celestial bodies as possibly being inhabited. Thus, without the Copernican revolution, it would not have been possible to consider other worlds as potentially being inhabited if the author's assumptions are true.


10. **Correct Answer:** No uninhabited world is the home of intelligent beings.

**Explanation:** The presence of intelligent beings is a necessary, but not sufficient, condition for a world to be inhabited; however, the passage also implies that the presence of intelligent beings on an inhabited world does not necessarily imply a lack of unintelligent ones as well. While this is most strongly suggested by the description of terrestrial explorers needing to find human beings in addition to plant and animal life, it is not precluded by the logical structure of the argument. The presence of intelligent life does not necessarily exclude the presence of non-intelligent life (A does not imply not-B), even if there is nothing in the passage that suggests that intelligent life requires non-intelligent life.

11. **Correct Answer:** An additional, secondary conclusion that can be derived from the primary conclusion of the passage

**Explanation:** The final sentence is a secondary conclusion based on one of the implications of the main conclusion of the section. As the primary conclusion states that all inhabited planets must have intelligent life with physical bodies, one may draw the subsequent conclusion that any inhabited planets must, as a necessary condition for these beings, meet certain conditions required by the bodies of living beings. This point is not so much the primary conclusion of the passage as it is an inference drawn from analyzing an assumption implicit in the necessary conditions for supporting certain kinds of life.

12. **Correct Answer:** Reflective and philosophical

**Explanation:** The author, who spends his first few paragraphs reflecting on the development of humanity's conception of the cosmos, adopts a philosophical point of view, examining the implications of these developments primarily from a metaphysical standpoint. While his tone is not especially emotional or passionate (ruling out many of the more extreme or emotionally charged options, like "witty" or "elegiac"), it is not overly detached and dry, like one would expect from "formal," "didactic," "objective," or "serious" writing.
The balanced, moderate, and reflective tone leads to choosing descriptors that are themselves neither overly intense nor overly removed in describing passion and emotion.

13. **Correct Answer:** As science has progressed, people have wondered if there are other worlds that might be inhabited by creatures like ourselves.

**Explanation:** The credited response is the only one that addresses the thesis of the passage as a whole, rather than the points of individual paragraphs or sections. While the other responses are supported by the passage, they do not capture the overall aim of the passage as a whole, which is what this particular type of question asks about. There are several parts and subsidiary ideas in this passage to look for in determining the credited response: the advancement of science, the conditions needed for a world to be considered inhabited, and how like human beings the inhabitants of other worlds must be. All of these are present in the correct response.

14. **Correct Answer:** Giving the history of the development of a theory; mentioning a consequence of this development; describing necessary conditions for a state of affairs; drawing conclusions from these conditions

**Explanation:** The credited response is the only one that describes the rhetorical and logical structure of the passage. The passage begins with a historical overview, before describing the scientific and philosophical consequences of the developments described in that overview. It then lays out the necessary conditions needed for a world to be considered inhabited before extrapolating conclusions from the consequences of these conditions. There is no mention of empirical scientific investigation based on observations, nor are there discussions of theoretical models, eliminating all responses that mention them.

15. **Correct Answer:** To transition between the historical and metaphysical survey of the opening paragraphs and the logical arguments of the following ones

**Explanation:** This paragraph is primarily a transition between the first and second sections of the passage. It attempts to connect the historical development of a contemporary problem— the controversy over the plurality of worlds—with some logical arguments that relate to that controversy, which is discussed in later paragraphs. By foreshadowing the eventual conclusion that will be argued for in the next paragraphs (inhabited worlds must contain intelligent creatures with physical bodies), the paragraph shows where the passage will eventually be heading. By mentioning the then-contemporary controversy of the plurality of worlds, it brings the historical sketch into the present, where it may be concluded, and by uniting the history of the first part of the passage and the logical arguments of the second part of the passage, it unites the two modes used in their respective sections and transitions from the one to the other.

# Practice Test 3: Text Completion

1 - The artist's approach was _____, blending classical techniques with modern themes to create works that resonated with diverse audiences.

**Choices**:
A) anachronistic
B) innovative
C) conventional
D) uninspired

2 - Despite numerous public debates, the policy _____ remained unchanged, which many criticized as a failure of the administration to respond to public demands.

**Choices**:

A) provisions
B) framework
C) agenda
D) stance


3 - Scientific consensus on climate change is _____; however, political responses vary greatly, from aggressive action to outright denial.

**Choices**:
A) equivocal
B) unanimous
C) divisive
D) robust


4 - Her approach to solving conflicts in the workplace was both _____ and effective, leading to significant improvements in team dynamics.

**Choices**:
A) dictatorial
B) judicious
C) haphazard
D) counterproductive


5 - As the debate progressed, the candidate's arguments became increasingly _____, straying from the main topic and confusing the audience.

**Choices**:
A) focused
B) tangential
C) pertinent
D) compelling


6 - The new regulation imposes _____ constraints on industrial emissions, which could force many companies to revamp their operational processes.

**Choices**:
A) negligible
B) stringent
C) flexible
D) outdated


7 - The philosopher's argument was _____, lacking sufficient evidence and relying too heavily on outdated studies.

**Choices**:
A) irrefutable
B) inconclusive
C) compelling
D) meticulous

8 - Her novel, while critically acclaimed, was _____ to many readers who found its narrative style overly complex and hard to follow.

**Choices**:
A) accessible
B) appealing
C) obscure
D) delightful

9 - Sentence: The theory of relativity, once _____ by the scientific community, now underpins fundamental concepts in physics and astronomy.

**Choices**:
A) disregarded
B) celebrated
C) embraced
D) questioned

10 - Sentence: Despite the company's recent success, its long-term sustainability remains _____ due to volatile market conditions and fluctuating consumer demands.

**Choices**:
A) assured
B) precarious
C) stagnant
D) unaffected

11 - Sentence: The professor's lecture on quantum mechanics was so _____ that even students unfamiliar with the basics could grasp the fundamental concepts.

**Choices**:
A) abstruse
B) accessible
C) esoteric
D) tedious

12 - Sentence: In medieval literature, dragons often symbolize _____ challenges that heroes must overcome to restore order and harmony.

**Choices**:
A) insurmountable
B) trivial
C) metaphorical
D) expected


13 - Sentence: The _____ growth of the tech industry has prompted many universities to expand their engineering programs to include cutting-edge technology and software development courses.

**Choices**:
A) stagnant
B) exponential
C) minimal
D) predicted


14 - Sentence: The critic's _____ review of the film, which highlighted its innovative use of animation and narrative depth, sparked widespread interest in its theatrical release.

**Choices**:
A) dismissive
B) lukewarm
C) laudatory
D) indifferent


15 - Sentence: The government's _____ response to the economic crisis, characterized by swift and decisive measures, helped stabilize the market and restore public confidence.

**Choices**:
A) delayed
B) tepid
C) prompt
D) haphazard


# Answer Sheet


1 - Sentence on the artist's approach:

**Correct Answer**: B) innovative

2 - Sentence on policy debate outcomes:

**Correct Answer**: D) stance

3 - Sentence on scientific consensus on climate change:

**Correct Answer**: C) divisive

4 - Sentence on conflict resolution in the workplace:

**Correct Answer**: B) judicious

5 - Sentence on the candidate's debate performance:

**Correct Answer**: B) tangential

6 - Sentence on new regulations for industrial emissions:

**Correct Answer**: B) stringent

7 - Sentence on the philosopher's argument:

**Correct Answer**: B) inconclusive

8 - Sentence on the readability of her novel:

**Correct Answer**: C) obscure

9 - Sentence of the theory of relativity:

**Correct Answer**: A) disregarded

10 - Sentence on the company's sustainability:

**Correct Answer**: B) precarious

11 - Sentence on the professor's lecture on quantum mechanics:

**Correct Answer**: B) accessible


12 - Sentence on dragons in medieval literature:

**Correct Answer**: C) metaphorical


13 - Sentence on the growth of the tech industry:

**Correct Answer:** B) exponential


14 - Sentence on the critic's review of the film:

**Correct Answer:** C) laudatory


15 - Sentence on the government's response to the economic crisis:

**Correct Answer**: C) prompt


# Practice Test 4: Sentence Equivalence


1 - The candidate's ability to _____ complex issues clearly and concisely during the debate helped her gain favor among undecided voters.

**Choices**:
A) obfuscate
B) elucidate
C) complicate
D) simplify


2 - Her memoir was _____, filled with vivid descriptions of her travels that brought distant cultures right to the reader's doorstep.

**Choices**:
A) evocative
B) insipid
C) dreary

D) enticing

3 - The new technology _____ the manufacturing process, significantly reducing the time it takes to produce a unit.

**Choices**:
A) streamlined
B) complicated
C) prolonged
D) expedited

4 - The political leader's promises _____ skepticism among the voters, many of whom had been disappointed by previous administrations.

**Choices**:
A) alleviated
B) engendered
C) dispelled
D) confirmed

5 - The _____ nature of the documentary, which covered several decades of history, captivated viewers with its depth and detail.

**Choices**:
A) fragmented
B) comprehensive
C) superficial
D) episodic

6 - His leadership style, known for being both _____ and effective, earned him respect even among his rivals.

**Choices**:
A) autocratic
B) authoritative
C) undisciplined
D) innovative

7 - The decision to _____ the old theater was met with both applause and outrage within the community.

**Choices**:
A) preserve

B) demolish
C) renovate
D) ignore

8 - The manager's ability to _____ conflicts has significantly improved the team's productivity and morale.

**Choices:**
A) exacerbate
B) resolve
C) overlook
D) provoke

9 - Sentence: The new policy on urban development was _____; it received as much praise for its innovation as it did criticism for its potential disruption to current housing markets.

**Choices:**
A) divisive
B) uncontroversial
C) welcomed
D) polarizing

10 - Sentence: The novelist's latest work was _____; readers found it either profoundly insightful or overly complex, with little middle ground.

**Choices:**
A) polarizing
B) enlightening
C) divisive
D) tedious
E) intriguing
F) monotonous

11 - Sentence: The CEO's strategy for turning around the company was _____, marked by a series of bold, albeit risky, decisions that ultimately paid off.

**Choices:**
A) conservative
B) audacious
C) cautious
D) daring
E) prudent
F) safe

12 - Sentence: The lecture on climate change was _____, filled with so much technical jargon that it was accessible only to specialists in the field.

**Choices**:
A) esoteric
B) abstruse
C) simplistic
D) understandable
E) clear
F) straightforward


13 - Sentence: The film's depiction of historical events was _____, sparking debate among historians about its accuracy and portrayal of real-life figures.

**Choices**:
A) fictionalized
B) accurate
C) authentic
D) controversial
E) distorted
F) precise


14 - Sentence: In his pursuit of happiness, he sought experiences that were _____, such as skydiving and deep-sea exploration.

**Choices**:
A) mundane
B) exhilarating
C) exciting
D) commonplace
E) thrilling
F) ordinary


15 - Sentence: The government's _____ approach to foreign policy has led to a more isolated position in international affairs.

**Choices**:
A) diplomatic
B) aggressive
C) conciliatory
D) isolated
E) unilateral

F) cooperative

# Answer Sheet

1 - Sentence on the candidate's debate performance:

**Correct Answer**: B) elucidate


2 - Sentence describing her memoir:

**Correct Answer**: A) evocative


3 - Sentence on the impact of new technology on manufacturing:

**Correct Answer**: A) streamlined


4 - Sentence on political leader's promises:

**Correct Answer**: B) engendered


5 - Sentence describing the documentary's nature:

**Correct Answer**: B) comprehensive


6 - Sentence describing his leadership style:

**Correct Answer**: D) innovative


7 - Sentence on the decision to alter the old theater:

**Correct Answer**: C) renovate


8 - Sentence on the manager's conflict resolution:

**Correct Answer**: B) resolve

9 - Sentence on the new policy on urban development

**Correct Answer**: D) polarizing


10 - Sentence on the novelist's latest work:

**Correct Answers**: A) polarizing, C) divisive


11 - Sentence on the CEO's strategy for turning around the company:

**Correct Answers**: B) audacious, D) daring


12 - Sentence on the lecture on climate change:

**Correct Answers**: A) esoteric, B) abstruse


13 - Sentence on the film's depiction of historical events:

**Correct Answers**: A) fictionalized, E) distorted


14 - Sentence on his pursuit of happiness through thrilling experiences:

**Correct Answers**: B) exhilarating, E) thrilling


15 - Sentence on the government's approach to foreign policy:

**Correct Answers**: E) unilateral, D) isolated


# Section-specific: Overview and Instructions of Quantitative Reasoning

Welcome to the Quantitative Reasoning section of your GRE practice tests. This part of the GRE is designed to measure your mathematical skills and your ability to analyze and interpret quantitative information. It consists of questions that require you to understand, interpret, and analyze quantitative information, solve problems using mathematical concepts, and apply basic skills and elementary concepts of arithmetic, algebra, geometry, and data analysis.

## Overview

**Content areas:** This section includes three types of questions: Quantitative Comparisons, Problem Solving, and Data Interpretation.

**Objective:** To assess your ability to reason quantitatively, solve quantitative problems, and interpret graphical data.

**Test format:** The Quantitative Reasoning section is split into two parts. The first part contains 12 questions with a 21-minute time allocation, and the second part consists of 15 questions with a 26-minute time allocation, totaling 27 questions to be completed in 47 minutes.

## Instructions for the Quantitative Reasoning Section

### Quantitative Comparisons

**Tasks:** You will compare two quantities and determine the relationship between them with the options being greater, lesser, equal, or indeterminate.

**Strategy:** Focus on understanding what is being asked and simplify the expressions or quantities where possible to make clear comparisons without unnecessary calculations.

### Problem Solving

**Tasks:** This involves solving mathematical problems presented either as word problems or as numeric calculations.

**Strategy:** Employ basic mathematical skills and consider quick estimation and elimination techniques to find solutions efficiently. Ensure you understand the problem fully before attempting to solve it.

### Data Interpretation

**Tasks:** These questions will ask you to interpret and analyze data given in graphs, tables, and other graphical formats to solve problems.

**Strategy:** Carefully analyze the given data, noting trends, comparing data points, and applying mathematical concepts to draw conclusions or predict outcomes.

### Timing and Pacing

**First section timing:** Allocate approximately 1.75 minutes per question in the first part. This allows time to review your calculations and ensure accuracy.

**Second section timing:** Provide slightly under 1.75 minutes per question in the second part. This pacing should help manage the slightly larger question volume.

**General time management:** Begin with the questions that seem most straightforward to you to secure quick wins and build confidence before moving on to more complex problems. Use any remaining time to check your answers, especially in questions involving multiple steps or calculations.

## Additional Tips

**Practice regularly:** Engage with a variety of question types and difficulty levels to become familiar with the range of topics and the styles of questions you will encounter.

**Mathematical review:** Regularly revisit fundamental mathematical concepts and formulas. Consistent practice with these basics can significantly enhance your speed and accuracy.

**Mock tests:** Taking timed practice tests will help you gauge your pacing and familiarize you with the pressure of working within the time limits of the actual exam.

By following these guidelines and regularly practicing, you will be well-prepared to tackle the Quantitative Reasoning section effectively, demonstrating your aptitude for quantitative analysis and problem-solving under timed conditions.

# Practice Test 5: Quantitative Comparisons

Here's a simulation of 15 Quantitative Comparisons questions for the GRE Quantitative Reasoning section. These questions test your ability to analyze and compare quantities quickly and accurately.

1
Quantity A: The sum of 3 consecutive positive even numbers.
Quantity B: The product of 2 and the smallest of the three numbers.

**Choices**:
A) Quantity A is greater
B) Quantity B is greater
C) The two quantities are equal
D) The relationship cannot be determined from the information given

2
Quantity A: $7^2$
Quantity B: 50

**Choices**:
A) Quantity A is greater
B) Quantity B is greater
C) The two quantities are equal
D) The relationship cannot be determined from the information given

3
Quantity A: The area of a circle with radius 4
Quantity B: The area of a square with side length 6

**Choices**:
A) Quantity A is greater
B) Quantity B is greater
C) The two quantities are equal
D) The relationship cannot be determined from the information given

4
Quantity A: The probability of drawing a red card from a standard deck of 52 cards
Quantity B: 0.5

**Choices**:
A) Quantity A is greater
B) Quantity B is greater
C) The two quantities are equal
D) The relationship cannot be determined from the information given

5
Quantity A: The volume of a sphere with radius 3
Quantity B: The volume of a cylinder with radius 3 and height 3

**Choices**:
A) Quantity A is greater
B) Quantity B is greater
C) The two quantities are equal
D) The relationship cannot be determined from the information given

6
Quantity A: The solution to the equation 2x - 4 = 10
Quantity B: 7

**Choices**:
A) Quantity A is greater
B) Quantity B is greater
C) The two quantities are equal
D) The relationship cannot be determined from the information given

7
Quantity A: The number of edges on a cube
Quantity B: The number of vertices on a cube

**Choices**:
A) Quantity A is greater
B) Quantity B is greater
C) The two quantities are equal

D) The relationship cannot be determined from the information given

8
Quantity A: Logarithm base 10 of 100
Quantity B: Logarithm base 10 of 1000

**Choices**:
A) Quantity A is greater
B) Quantity B is greater
C) The two quantities are equal
D) The relationship cannot be determined from the information given

9
Quantity A: The integer part of $(2,99)^3$
Quantity B: 24

**Choices**:
A) Quantity A is greater
B) Quantity B is greater
C) The two quantities are equal
D) The relationship cannot be determined from the information given

10
Quantity A: 15% of 80
Quantity B: 10% of 120

**Choices**:
A) Quantity A is greater
B) Quantity B is greater
C) The two quantities are equal
D) The relationship cannot be determined from the information given

11
Quantity A: The sum of angles in a triangle
Quantity B: 180 degrees

**Choices**:
A) Quantity A is greater
B) Quantity B is greater
C) The two quantities are equal
D) The relationship cannot be determined from the information given

12
Quantity A: The length of the diagonal of a square with side length 5
Quantity B: 7

**Choices**:
A) Quantity A is greater

B) Quantity B is greater
C) The two quantities are equal
D) The relationship cannot be determined from the information given

13
Quantity A: The number of prime numbers less than 20
Quantity B: The number of even numbers between 1 and 20

**Choices**:
A) Quantity A is greater
B) Quantity B is greater
C) The two quantities are equal
D) The relationship cannot be determined from the information given

14
Quantity A: The factorial of 4 (4!)
Quantity B: The square of 4 ($4^2$)

**Choices**:
A) Quantity A is greater
B) Quantity B is greater
C) The two quantities are equal
D) The relationship cannot be determined from the information given

15
Quantity A: The sum of the first 10 positive integers
Quantity B: The sum of the first 5 positive even numbers

**Choices**:
A) Quantity A is greater
B) Quantity B is greater
C) The two quantities are equal
D) The relationship cannot be determined from the information given

These questions are designed to reflect the typical structure and challenge of GRE Quantitative Comparisons questions, allowing you to test your mathematical reasoning and your ability to compare quantities effectively.

# Answer Sheet

**1 - Correct Answer**: A) Quantity A is greater

**Explanation**: The sum of 3 consecutive even numbers is three times the middle number, which is always greater than twice the smallest number.

**2 - Correct Answer**: B) Quantity B is greater

**Explanation**: $7^2 = 49$, which is less than 50.


**3 - Correct Answer**: A) Quantity A is greater

**Explanation**: The area of a circle with radius 4 is $16\pi$, and the area of a square with side 6 is 36. Since $\pi = 3.1416, 16\pi > 36$


**4 - Correct Answer**: C) The two quantities are equal

**Explanation**: The probability of drawing a red card from a standard deck is exactly 0.5.


**5 - Correct Answer**: A) Quantity A is greater

**Explanation**: The volume of a sphere with radius 3 is $36\pi$, and the volume of a cylinder with radius 3 and height 3 is $27\pi$, thus the cylinder has less volume.


**6 - Correct Answer**: C) The two quantities are equal

**Explanation**: Solving $2x - 4 = 10$ gives $x = 7$, so Quantity A, 7, equals Quantity B, 7.


**7 - Correct Answer**: A) Quantity A is greater

**Explanation**: A cube has 12 edges and 8 vertices.


**8 - Correct Answer**: B) Quantity B is greater

**Explanation:** $log_{10}(100) = 2$ and $log_{10}(1000) = 3$


**9 - Correct Answer**: A) Quantity A is greater

**Explanation**: $(2.99)^3$ is slightly less than 27, making it around 26 when considering the integer part, which is greater than 24.


**10 - Correct Answer**: C) The two quantities are equal

**Explanation**: 15% of 80 is 12 and 10% of 120 is 12; hence, they are equal.

**11 - Correct Answer**: C) The two quantities are equal

**Explanation**: The sum of angles in a triangle is always 180°.


**12 - Correct Answer**: A) Quantity A is greater

**Explanation**: The diagonal of a square with side length 5 is $5\sqrt{2}$ which is approximately 7.07, so Quantity B, 7, is slightly lesser.


**13 - Correct Answer**: B) Quantity B is greater

**Explanation**: There are 8 prime numbers less than 20 and 10 even numbers between 1 and 20.


**14 - Correct Answer**: A) Quantity A is greater

**Explanation**: 4! (factorial of 4) is 24 and $4^2$ (square of 4) is 16.


**15 - Correct Answer**: A) Quantity A is greater

**Explanation**: The sum of the first 10 positive integers is 55, and the sum of the first 5 positive even numbers is 30.


# Practice Test 6: Problem solving


**1 - Question**: If x+y = 10 and xy =24, what is $x^2 + y^2$?

**Choices**:
A) 52
B) 64
C) 76
D) 100


**2 - Question**: A bag contains 3 red, 4 blue, and 5 green marbles. If two marbles are picked at random, what is the probability that both are green?

**Choices**:

A) $\frac{5}{33}$

B) $\frac{2}{11}$

C) $\frac{1}{4}$

D) $\frac{2}{5}$

**3 - Question**: What is the area of a triangle with base 8 cm and height 9 cm?

**Choices**:
A) 36 cm²
B) 72 cm²
C) 18 cm²
D) 64 cm²

**4 - Question**: If $5x - 3 = 2x + 7$, then x = ?

**Choices**:
A) 2
B) 3.33
C) 4
D) 5

**5 - Question**: A train traveling at a constant speed covers the distance between two cities in 45 minutes. If the speed of the train had been increased by 10 km/h, it would have taken 36 minutes. What is the distance between the two cities?

**Choices**:
A) 54 km
B) 60 km
C) 72 km
D) 90 km

**6 - Question**: In a certain school, the ratio of boys to girls is 3:4. If there are 600 students in the school, how many are boys?

**Choices**:
A) 225
B) 250
C) 257

D) 300

**7 - Question:** A rectangular park 50 m long and 30 m wide is surrounded by a walking path of uniform width. If the total area of the park and path is 2240 m², what is the width of the path?

**Choices:**
A) 2 m
B) 4 m
C) 5 m
D) 6 m

**8 - Question:** If the sum of the interior angles of a polygon is 1260 degrees, how many sides does the polygon have?

**Choices:**
A) 9
B) 10
C) 8
D) 7

**9 - Question:** A company sells its product at $15 per unit. The fixed costs are $300, and the variable cost per unit is $10. How many units must the company sell to break even?

**Choices:**
A) 30
B) 50
C) 60
D) 75

**10 - Question:** If the price of a shirt after a 20% discount is $48, what was the original price?

**Choices:**
A) $58
B) $60
C) $64
D) $72

**11 - Question:** The sequence of numbers 1, 5, 14, 30, 55,... What is the next number in the sequence?

**Choices:**
A) 85
B) 91

C) 78
D) 105


**12 - Question**: A cyclist travels 45 km in 3 hours. What is the average speed of the cyclist in km/h?

**Choices**:
A) 12 km/h
B) 15 km/h
C) 18 km/h
D) 20 km/h


**13 - Question**: If $3^x = 81$, what is the value of x?

**Choices**:
A) 2
B) 3
C) 4
D) 5


**14 - Question**: A shop offers a 25% discount on all items. If an item originally costs $80, what is the discount price?

**Choices**:
A) $60
B) $65
C) $20
D) $55


**15 - Question**: The angles in a quadrilateral are in the ratio 2:3:5:8. What is the measure of the largest angle?

**Choices:**
A) 144 degrees
B) 160 degrees
C) 120 degrees
D) 100 degrees


These questions encompass a comprehensive range of types and difficulties, designed to prepare students effectively for the quantitative reasoning problems they will encounter on the GRE.

# Answer Sheet

1 - Question on consecutive even numbers:

**Correct Answer**: A) 52

**Explanation**: $x^2 + y^2 = (x + y)^2 - 2xy = 100 - 48 = 52$

2 - Question on probability with marbles:

**Correct Answer**: A) $\frac{5}{33}$

**Explanation**: Probability = $\frac{\frac{5}{2}}{\frac{12}{2}} = \frac{10}{66} = \frac{5}{33}$ (Note: use permutation formula numerator & denominator)

3 - Question on the area of a triangle:

**Correct Answer**: A) 36 cm²

**Explanation**: Area = $\frac{1}{2} \times 8 \times 9 = 36$

4 - Question on solving an equation:

**Correct Answer**: B) 3.33

**Explanation**: Solving $5x - 3 = 2x + 7$ gives $x = 10/3$

5 - Question on train travel time and speed:

**Correct Answer**: D) 30 km

**Explanation**: Using the distance formula d = t × v, the distance equals 30 km when recalculated with the new speed and time and equating both equations.

6 - Question on ratio of boys to girls:

**Correct Answer**: C) 257

**Explanation**: Boys = $\frac{3}{7}$ × 600 = 257

7 - Question on area of a park and path:

**Correct Answer**: B) 4 m

**Explanation**: Solving (50 + 2w)(30 + 2w) = 2240 gives; w=4

8 - Question on sides of a polygon:

**Correct Answer**: A) 9

**Explanation**: 180(n − 2) = 1260 solves to n = 9

9 - Question on break-even units:

**Correct Answer**: C) 60

**Explanation**: Break-even point = $\frac{300}{15-10}$ = 60

10 - Question on original price of a shirt:

**Correct Answer**: B) $60

**Explanation**: P − 0.2P = 48, solving for P gives P=60

11 - Question on a number sequence:

**Correct Answer**: B) 91

**Explanation**: Pattern suggests adding consecutive odd numbers starting from 4. Next number is 55 + 36 = 91

12 - Question on average speed of a cyclist:

**Correct Answer**: B) 15 km/h

**Explanation**: 45 ÷ 3 = 15

13 - Question on solving for x in an exponential equation:

**Correct Answer:** C) 4

**Explanation**: $3^4 = 81$

14 - Question on discount price of an item:

**Correct Answer**: A) $60

**Explanation**: $80 - 0.25 \times 80 = 60$

15 - Question on angles in a quadrilateral:

**Correct Answer:** B) 160 degrees

**Explanation**: Ratio total is 18; largest angle $= \frac{8}{18} \times 360 = 160$

# Practice Test 7: Data Interpretation

Here's a set of 15 Data Interpretation questions for the GRE Quantitative Reasoning section, designed to assess your ability to analyze and interpret data from various graphical and tabular sources. These questions are crafted to mirror the complexity and diversity of scenarios you might encounter on the actual GRE exam.

**1 - Graph Type**: Line Graph

**Data Content**: Monthly sales of a company over one year, showing significant fluctuations.

**Question**: In which month did the company experience the highest sales increase compared to the previous month?

**Choices**:
A) March
B) June
C) September
D) December

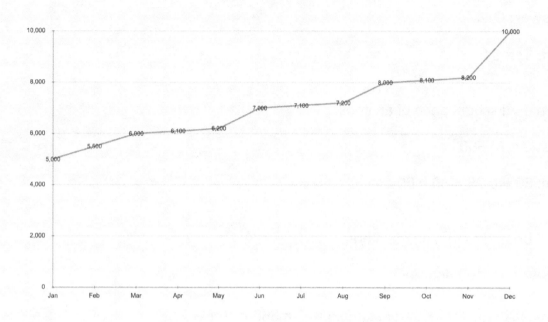

**2 - Table Content**: Multi-year comparison of R&D investment as a percentage of revenue for tech companies.

**Question**: Which company showed the greatest year-over-year variability in its R&D investment ratio?

**Choices**:
A) TechCorp
B) InnovateInc
C) SoftSolutions
D) HardwareHub

| Year | TechCorp (%) | InnovateInc (%) | SoftSolutions (%) | HardwareHub (%) |
|------|--------------|-----------------|-------------------|-----------------|
| 2015 | 5.5 | 6.2 | 4.8 | 3.3 |
| 2016 | 5.7 | 7.0 | 5.0 | 3.5 |
| 2017 | 6.4 | 8.1 | 5.2 | 3.7 |
| 2018 | 6.1 | 8.5 | 4.9 | 3.8 |
| 2019 | 7.0 | 7.8 | 5.4 | 4.2 |
| 2020 | 7.2 | 6.5 | 5.5 | 4.5 |

**3 - Graph Type**: Waterfall Chart

**Data Content**: Fiscal year breakdown of a company's revenue streams and expenditures leading to net income.

**Question**: Determine the expense category that most significantly eroded gross profits.

**Choices**:
A) Production Costs
B) Marketing Spend
C) R&D Investment
D) Administrative Expenses

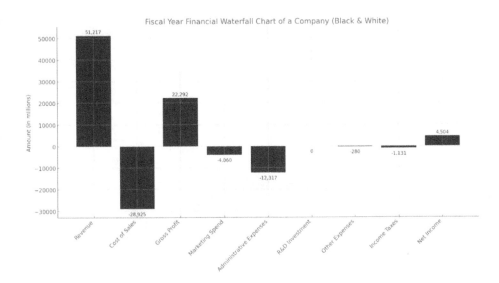

Fiscal Year Financial Waterfall Chart of a Company (Black & White)

**4 - Graph Type:** 3D Surface Plot

**Data Content:** A 3D Surface Plot depicting profitability based on varying levels of production volume (X-axis) and pricing strategy (Y-axis) across four quarters (Q1 to Q4).

**Question**: Identify the quarter and price-volume combination where the company reached peak profitability.

**Choices**:
A) Q1 at high volume-low price
B) Q2 at medium volume-medium price
C) Q3 at low volume-high price
D) Q4 at high volume-high price

Q1 Profitability Surface

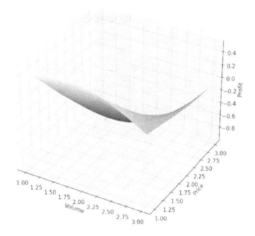

Q2 Profitability Surface

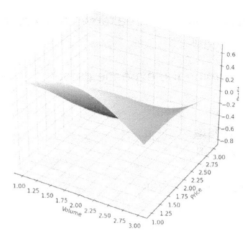

Q3 Profitability Surface

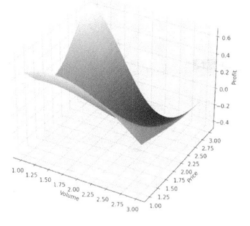

Q4 Profitability Surface

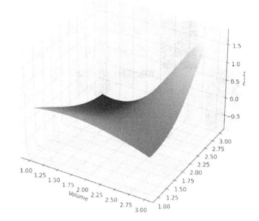

**5 - Graph Type**: Pie chart

**Data Content:** A complex pie chart detailing the percentage distribution of a national budget into sectors such as healthcare, education, defense, and infrastructure, with smaller slices for other miscellaneous sectors.

**Question:** Which sector, excluding the top three, shows the largest percentage point increase in allocation from the previous year's budget?

**Choices**:
A) Healthcare
B) Education
C) Defense
D) Infrastructure

106

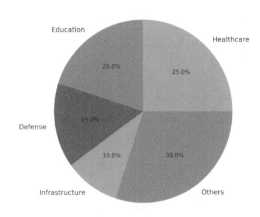 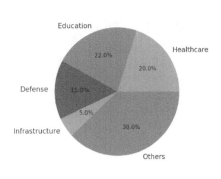

**6 - Graph Type**: Pareto chart

**Data Content:** A Pareto chart analyzing customer feedback issues, ranking them from most to least frequent, and categorizing them by department (Customer Service, Billing, Technical Support).

**Question**: Determine the category that accounts for the smallest proportion of issues but is the second most frequent complaint within a single department.

**Choices**:
A) Customer Service
B) Billing
C) Technical Support
D) Shipping

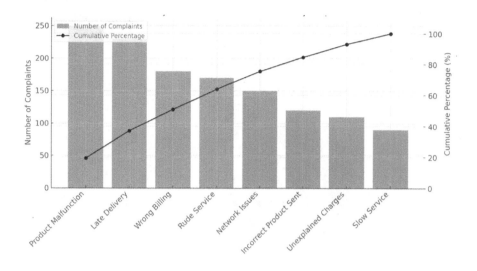

**7 - Graph Type**: Multi-axis chart

**Data Content**: A multi-axis chart plotting the ROI of marketing campaigns on one axis and customer acquisition costs on the other, over four quarters.
Question: In which quarter does the data indicate an optimal balance between ROI and acquisition cost?

**Choices:**
A) Q1
B) Q2
C) Q3
D) Q4

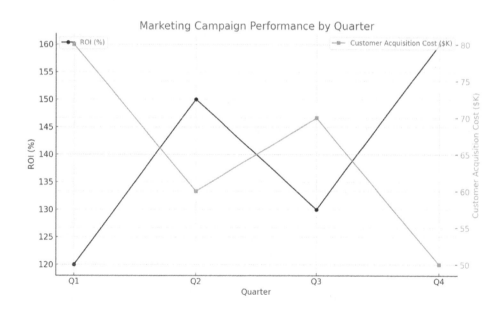

**8 - Graph Type**: Multi-Variable Box Plot

**Data Content**: Distribution of sale prices for three different housing types (Single Family, Condo, Townhouse) in five urban regions.

**Question**: In which housing type and urban region combination is the interquartile range the narrowest, indicating a stable market?

**Choices**:
A) Single Family in Region 1
B) Condo in Region 3
C) Townhouse in Region 2
D) Condo in Region 5

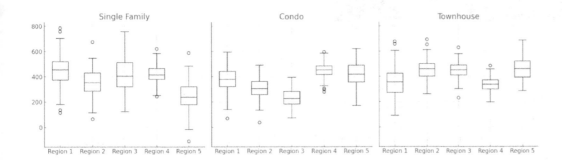

**9 - Graph Type**: Heat Map

**Data Content**: Correlation matrix of investment returns for different asset classes (Equities, Bonds, Real Estate, Commodities, Cash) over a ten-year period.

**Question**: Identify the pair of asset classes that exhibit the least correlation over the ten-year period.

**Choices**:
A) Equities and Bonds
B) Real Estate and Commodities
C) Commodities and Cash
D) Bonds and Real Estate

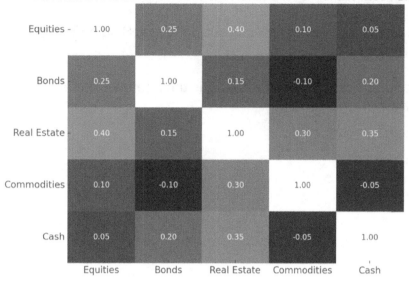

Correlation Matrix of Investment Returns for Different Asset Classes

**10 - Graph Type**: Mixed-Line and Bar Graph

**Data Content:** Year-on-year inflation rate (line graph) and consumer confidence index (bar graph) over ten years.

**Question**: Identify the year when a sharp increase in the inflation rate was counterintuitively accompanied by a rise in consumer confidence.

**Choices**:
A) 2012
B) 2015
C) 2018
D) 2020

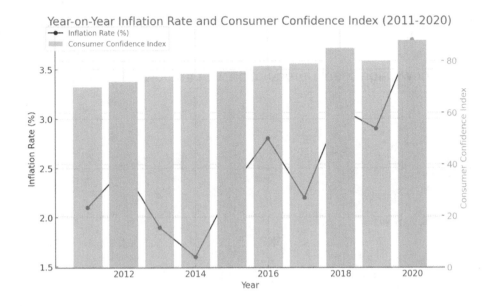

**11 - Graph Type**: Histogram with a Normal Distribution Curve

**Data Content**: Distribution of scores from a national standardized test.

**Question**: Assess where the 90th percentile falls within the distribution of scores.

**Choices**:
A) Below the mean
B) Within one standard deviation above the mean
C) Between one and two standard deviations above the mean
D) More than two standard deviations above the mean

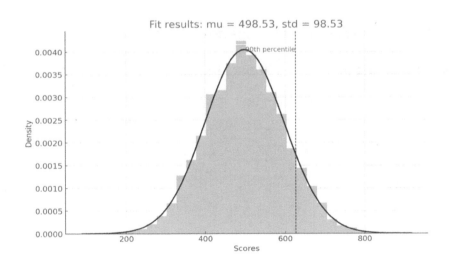

**12 - Graph Type**: Volcano Plot

**Data Content:** Gene expression levels measured by fold change and p-value from a clinical trial study.

**Question:** Identify the gene that shows significant upregulation with the lowest p-value.

**Choices:**
A) Gene A
B) Gene B
C) Gene C
D) Gene D

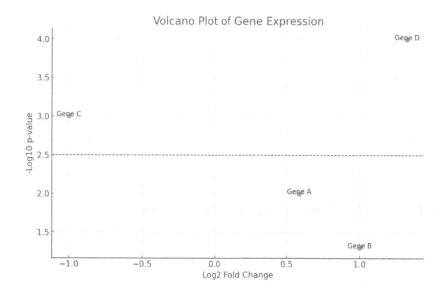

**13 - Graph Type:** Tornado Diagram

**Data Content:** Sensitivity analysis for a financial model assessing project risk factors.

**Question:** Which risk factor has the greatest potential to impact the project's net present value (NPV)?

**Choices:**
A) Interest Rate Fluctuations
B) Material Cost Variability
C) Labor Market Uncertainty
D) Regulatory Changes

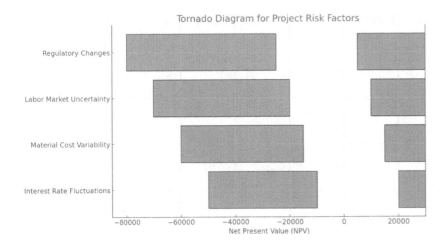

Tornado Diagram for Project Risk Factors

**14 - Graph Type**: Stream Graph

**Data Content**: Website traffic sources (organic, direct, referral, social media) over 12 months.

**Question**: In which month did referral traffic peak, and what was the consequent effect on the other traffic sources?

**Choices**:
A) January
B) April
C) July
D) February

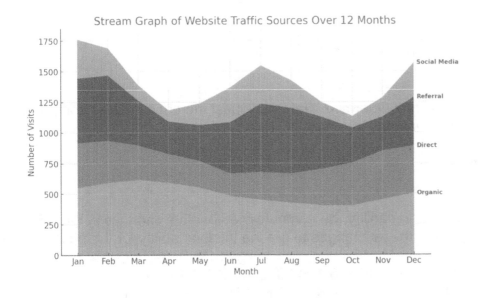

**15 - Graph Type:** Alluvial Flow Diagram

**Data Content**: Employee career path movements within a company over five years, categorized by department.

**Question**: From which department did the largest number of employees transition into management roles?

**Choices**:
A) Research and Development
B) Sales and Marketing
C) Operations
D) Customer Service

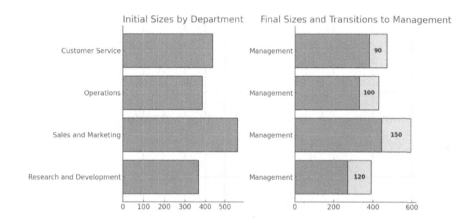

# Answer Sheet

1 - Upon examining the graph, you can determine that the highest increase in sales compared to the previous month occurred in December.

**Correct answer**: D) December

2 - To determine the year-over-year variability, we compute the absolute changes in the R&D investment ratio each year and sum these changes to get the total variability for the period:

TechCorp Variability: $|5.7-5.5|+|6.4-5.7|+|6.1-6.4|+|7.0-6.1|+|7.2-7.0| = 1.6$
InnovateInc Variability: $|7.0-6.2|+|8.1-7.0|+|8.5-8.1|+|7.8-8.5|+|6.5-7.8| = 5.0$
SoftSolutions Variability: $|5.0-4.8|+|5.2-5.0|+|4.9-5.2|+|5.4-4.9|+|5.5-5.4| = 1.1$
HardwareHub Variability: $|3.5-3.3|+|3.7-3.5|+|3.8-3.7|+|4.2-3.8|+|4.5-4.2| = 1.7$

Based on the calculations:

114

InnovateInc showed the greatest year-over-year variability in its R&D investment ratio with a total variability of 5.0%.

**Correct Answer**: B) InnovateInc

3 - Based on the chart, the Administrative Expenses category most significantly eroded gross profits compared to Production Costs, Marketing Spend, and R&D Investment.

**Correct Answer**: D) Administrative Expenses

4 - Based on the peak values calculated from the profitability function for each quarter:
Q1 peak profitability: 0.54
Q2 peak profitability: 0.70
Q3 peak profitability: 0.67
Q4 peak profitability: 1.86
The highest peak profitability occurs in Q4

**Correct Answer:** Q4 at high volume-high price

5 - From the percentage point changes calculated:
Healthcare: +5%
Education: -2%
Defense: 0%
Infrastructure: +5%
Others: -8%
Among the sectors listed in the choices (Healthcare, Education, Defense, Infrastructure), excluding the top three overall sectors by percentage (Healthcare, Education, Defense based on their prominence), Infrastructure shows the largest percentage point increase in allocation from the previous year's budget (+5%).

**Correct Answer**: D) Infrastructure

6 - From the data processed, the ranking of issues within each department reveals:

Technical Support: 'Product Malfunction' and 'Network Issues' are the top two issues.
Billing: 'Wrong Billing' and 'Unexplained Charges' are the top two issues.

Customer Service: 'Rude Service' and 'Slow Service' are the top two issues.

Shipping: 'Late Delivery' and 'Incorrect Product Sent' are the top two issues.
The question asks for the category that accounts for the smallest proportion of overall issues but is the second most frequent complaint within a single department. Analyzing the data, Billing with 'Unexplained Charges' fits this criterion best. 'Unexplained Charges' is the second

most frequent complaint within the Billing department, and compared to other second-place complaints in other departments, it holds a smaller proportion of the overall issue count.

**Correct Answer**: B) Billing


7 - From the analysis, the balance scores for each quarter, calculated as the ratio of ROI to acquisition cost, are as follows:

Q1: 1.5
Q2: 2.5
Q3: 1.86
Q4: 3.2

The highest balance score occurs in Q4, where the ROI is at its peak and the acquisition cost is at its lowest compared to the other quarters. This indicates that Q4 achieves the best balance between high ROI and low customer acquisition cost, making it the optimal choice.

**Correct Answer**: D) Q4


8 - From the calculated IQRs for each housing type and region combination:

Condo in Region 3: IQR ≈ 100.24
Condo in Region 5: IQR ≈ 134.99
Single Family in Region 1: IQR ≈ 147.87
Townhouse in Region 2: IQR ≈ 100.39

The narrowest IQR, indicating the most stable market, is for Condo in Region 4 with an IQR of approximately 68.37. This suggests that the market for condos in Region 4 is the most stable among the options given due to the smallest variability in sale prices.

However, since Condo in Region 4 is not one of the given choices in the question, among the available options, Condo in Region 3 has the narrowest IQR of the listed choices and would be considered the most stable market for those options.

**Correct Answer**: B) Condo in Region 3


9 - From the correlation values extracted for the specific pairs given in the choices:

A) Equities and Bonds: 0.25
B) Real Estate and Commodities: 0.30
C) Commodities and Cash: -0.05
D) Bonds and Real Estate: 0.15

The pair that exhibits the least correlation over the ten-year period, based on the given choices, is C) Commodities and Cash with a correlation coefficient of -0.05. This negative value indicates not just low correlation but a slight inverse relationship, meaning as one asset class increases in value, the other tends to decrease, and vice versa.

**Correct Answer**: C) Commodities and Cash

10 - Based on the analysis of data:

In 2012, the inflation rate increased to 2.5% from the previous year's 2.1%, and consumer confidence rose to 72 from 70.
In 2015, the inflation rate rose to 2.3% from 1.6% in the previous year, and consumer confidence increased to 76 from 75.
In 2018, there was a more notable increase in the inflation rate to 3.1% from 2.2% in 2017, and consumer confidence rose significantly to 85 from 79.
In 2020, the inflation rate jumped to 3.8% from 2.9% in 2019, and consumer confidence increased to 88 from 80.

Among these, 2018 represents a year when a sharp increase in the inflation rate was counterintuitively accompanied by a significant rise in consumer confidence. The increase in both metrics during 2018 is more pronounced compared to other years, making it a standout year for this trend.

**Correct Answer**: C) 2018

11 - The histogram with a normal distribution curve above displays the distribution of scores from a national standardized test. The curve fits the histogram data, indicating the typical bell-shaped curve of a normal distribution. The mean ($\mu$) is approximately 500 and the standard deviation ($\sigma$) is about 100.

The 90th percentile, marked with a dashed line, falls between one and two standard deviations above the mean. This is visually evident from the graph and aligns with statistical norms where the 90th percentile typically falls around the value of $\mu + 1.28\sigma$.

**Correct Answer**: C) Between one and two standard deviations above the mean

12 - The volcano plot above visualizes gene expression levels, showing both fold change (on a log2 scale) and significance (as the negative log of the p-value). Each gene is represented by a point on the plot, with significant genes labeled directly on the graph.

In this case, Gene D exhibits significant upregulation and possesses the lowest p-value among the significant genes, as evidenced by its placement farthest along the y-axis (which measures the negative log of the p-value), surpassing the set threshold for significance.

**Correct Answer**: D) Gene D

13 - The tornado diagram above visualizes the sensitivity analysis for various risk factors affecting a financial model's net present value (NPV). Each horizontal bar represents the potential increase and decrease in NPV due to changes in each risk factor, with the base-case NPV indicated by a vertical line.

From the analysis, Interest Rate Fluctuations show the greatest range of impact on the project's NPV, with the highest potential increase and a significant decrease. This range is larger compared to other factors, indicating that changes in interest rates have the most substantial potential to impact the project's financial outcome.

**Correct Answer**: A) Interest Rate Fluctuations


14 - The stream graph above visually represents the flow of website traffic sources (organic, direct, referral, social media) over 12 months. Each wavy layer corresponds to one traffic source, and the fluctuations in the graph show how each source varies over time.

From the analysis, referral traffic peaked in February.

**Correct Answer**: D) February


15 - The generated diagram visually simulates an alluvial flow diagram using horizontal bar charts to represent the transitions of employees from their initial departments into management roles. Each department's initial and final sizes are shown, along with the number of employees transitioning to management, depicted as lighter segments on the right-hand side of the graph.
From the analysis Sales and Marketing had the largest number of employees (150) transition into management roles, as indicated by the largest lighter segment on the right-side graph.

**Correct Answer**: B) Sales and Marketing


# Full-length simulated exam practice tests: Overview and Instructions


Welcome to the first full-length practice test of our series, designed to mirror the updated structure of the GRE, effective from September 2023. This revised version of the GRE has been streamlined to enhance the testing experience, reducing the total exam time and modifying the structure of the sections without altering the type of questions. Here you will find a comprehensive simulation that reflects these changes, providing an accurate feel for the new test format. Below are the instructions and an overview to guide you through this simulated exam.

## Overview

This practice test is structured to reflect the revised GRE, which now includes fewer questions and one less analytical writing task, allowing the entire exam to be completed in just under two hours. The sections included in this test are Analytical Writing, Verbal Reasoning, and Quantitative Reasoning, structured as follows:

**Analytical Writing:** This section now includes only one task, "Analyze an Issue," with a duration of 30 minutes.

**Verbal Reasoning:** Consisting of two sections—12 questions and 15 questions—to be completed in 41 minutes.

**Quantitative Reasoning:** Also comprising two sections—12 questions and 15 questions—with a time allotment of 47 minutes.

## Instructions for Taking the Test

**Prepare your environment:** Ensure that you are in a quiet, interruption-free environment that mimics the conditions of a test center as closely as possible.

**Timing:** Strictly adhere to the timing for each section as specified. Use a timer to ensure you are working within the new time constraints of the GRE, which are critical to successfully completing the test.

**Allowed materials:** You may use scratch paper and pencils for note-taking and calculations. For the Quantitative Reasoning section, a basic on-screen calculator will be available, similar to the actual GRE.

**Scheduled breaks:** The revised GRE format includes no scheduled breaks due to the shorter test duration. Ensure you are prepared to complete the test without breaks, mimicking the continuous testing environment.

**Answering strategy:** Attempt all questions as there is no penalty for incorrect answers. Mark questions you find challenging and may wish to review if time allows, but ensure you provide an answer before moving on.

**Scoring:** After completing the test, use the answer key provided to score your test. This will be crucial for assessing your readiness and identifying areas where further review is required.

## Effective Test-Taking Tips

**Pace yourself:** Given the shorter duration of each section, it's vital to keep track of the time to ensure that you can answer all questions.

**Read instructions carefully:** Familiarize yourself with the instructions for each section before beginning, to avoid simple mistakes.

**Practice efficiently:** Since the type of questions remains unchanged, focus on answering efficiently under the new timing constraints.

This complete simulation is crafted to reflect the significant changes in the GRE format introduced in September 2023. By taking this practice test seriously and adhering to the new conditions, you will gain valuable insight into your preparation levels and areas needing improvement. Good luck, and remember that understanding the new structure and adapting your test-taking strategies accordingly are key to success on the GRE.

# Practice Test 8: Complete Simulation

## Analytical Writing: Issue Task Simulation

### Instructions

You will be given a statement about a general interest topic. Your task is to write a well-organized essay in which you explain the extent to which you agree or disagree with the statement and support your viewpoint with reasons and examples.

**Time allowed:** 30 minutes

### Issue Prompt

"Technology ultimately separates and alienates people more than it serves to bring them together."

### Task

Write a response in which you discuss the extent to which you agree or disagree with the statement above. In developing and supporting your position, you should consider ways in which the statement might or might not hold true and explain how these considerations shape your position.

### Points to Consider

1. **Impact on communication:** Reflect on how technology—through social media, instant messaging, and email—has changed the ways people communicate. Does it enhance connections or create a superficial level of interaction that may undermine real personal connections?
2. **Work environments:** Consider the role technology plays in work environments, especially with the rise of remote working and teleconferencing. Has technology made collaborative work easier and more productive, or has it led to isolation and a lack of real teamwork?
3. **Social dynamics:** Think about the broader social implications, such as the role of technology in creating or bridging cultural divides. Does technology promote inclusivity and understanding among different groups, or does it lead to echo chambers and increased polarization?

4. **Personal experiences:** You may draw on personal experiences where technology either helped you connect with others in meaningful ways or instances where it felt isolating.

## Writing Tips

**Introduction:** Briefly introduce your viewpoint on the issue. State whether you agree or disagree with the prompt, and summarize the main reasons for your position.

**Body paragraphs:** Each paragraph should focus on a specific reason or example supporting your viewpoint. Use clear topic sentences, and provide concrete examples or data where possible.

**Counterarguments:** Consider acknowledging a counterargument to show that you have thought about the issue from multiple perspectives. Explain why this counterargument does not change your overall position.

**Conclusion:** Summarize your argument and reinforce how the examples you provided support your viewpoint.

# Verbal Reasoning: Reading Comprehension Task Simulation

**Passage:**

To create the Trafficking in Persons (TIPS) Report, the Secretary of State ranks countries according to a system of tiers based on the efforts those countries make against human trafficking. According to the United States, the minimum conditions that a country must meet to be a country in good standing, designated as a Tier 1 country, are somewhat subjective. There must be "serious and sustained efforts to eliminate human trafficking," such as prohibiting and punishing acts of human trafficking, taking measures to deter offenses in the future, creating public awareness, and protecting victims of human trafficking.

Tier 2 countries do not fully comply with the standards for Tier 1 countries, but are making significant efforts to do so. Tier 2 Watch List countries meet the same criteria as Tier 2 countries, but also satisfy one of the following: 1) the number of victims of severe forms of trafficking is very significant or significantly increasing; 2) no evidence can be shown that there are increasing efforts to combat severe forms of trafficking in persons from the previous year; or 3) the finding that a country was making significant efforts to comply with minimum standards was based on that country's commitment to take future steps over the next year. Tier 3 countries do not fully comply with the minimum standards and are not making significant efforts to do so. The penalties for Tier 3 countries include being subject to certain sanctions such as: the withdrawal of non-humanitarian and non-trade related foreign assistance, not receiving funding for educational and cultural exchange programs, and potential U.S. opposition to assistance from international financial institutions such as the World Bank and International Monetary Fund.

The TIPS Report relies on U.S. missions to regularly meet with foreign government officials in order to gain information about human trafficking in countries throughout the world. It is the world's most comprehensive report on human trafficking, and is trusted as an accurate depiction of the policies and laws being used in various countries. Specifically, the TIPS Report evaluates countries' efforts against human trafficking based on the efforts taken in the areas of prosecution, prevention, and protection. The evaluation of a country's prosecution efforts is based on whether laws against human trafficking exist and are actively enforced against perpetrators. Prevention efforts should focus on raising public awareness about human trafficking and rectifying laws that make certain populations more vulnerable to human trafficking than others. Finally, protection efforts seek to address the needs of existing or potential victims.

**Questions:**

1. It can be inferred from the passage that the primary purpose of the TIPS report is to:

   A. Provide a consistent system for documenting how various countries respond to the issue of human trafficking
   B. Enable to the United States to exercise its power in the arena of humanitarian affairs
   C. Discourage countries from passively accepting the levels of human trafficking within their borders
   D. Motivate countries to implement methods that fight human trafficking by using the prevention, protection and prosecution techniques
   E. Create a system of incentives for countries to fight human trafficking, while also tracking which countries are effectively addressing the issue

2. The author most likely provides an explanation of the tier system used by the TIPS Report in order to:

   A. Show how the United States ranks countries' efforts to combat human trafficking
   B. Simplify a complex problem
   C. Highlight the drastic differences in how human trafficking is addressed throughout the world
   D. Minimize the severity of a serious issue
   E. Demonstrate that different countries handle human trafficking in different ways

3. The primary purpose of the passage is most likely to

   A. Describe a type of report produced by the United States
   B. Shed light on a complex issue
   C. Describe the evolution of a program
   D. Compare and contrast different forms of measurement
   E. Quantify a qualitative issue

4. Which one of the following best captures the author's attitude toward the TIPS Report?

    A. Subtly emotive, as the text deals with a sensitive issue
    B. Disinterested in the human trauma that results from human trafficking
    C. Enthusiasm for its effectiveness and innovative tactics
    D. Objectively descriptive of how the TIPS Report is used to assess countries' actions against human trafficking
    E. Admiration for the TIPS Report's ability to be nonpartisan


5. Which of the following is NOT a penalty that a Tier 3 country might be subject to?

    A. Being punished by the World Bank
    B. Withdrawal of funding for cultural exchange programs
    C. Reduction in funding for educational programs
    D. U.S. opposition to assistance from the International Monetary Fund
    E. Withdrawal of non-trade related foreign assistance


6. The author mentions that U.S. missions regularly meet with foreign officials for all of the reasons EXCEPT:

    A. To help cast the TIPS Report in a positive light
    B. To suggest that the TIPS Report is politically biased
    C. To demonstrate that the U.S. is willing to engage in dialogue with other countries
    D. To demonstrate a willingness on the part of the United States to cooperate with other countries
    E. To offer insight as to how data is collected


**Passage:**

1. OBJECTS OF HUMAN KNOWLEDGE. It is evident to anyone who takes a survey of the objects of human knowledge, that they are either IDEAS actually imprinted on the senses; or else such as are perceived by attending to the passions and operations of the mind; or lastly, ideas formed by help of memory and imagination—either compounding, dividing, or barely representing those originally perceived in the aforesaid ways. By sight I have the ideas of light and colors, with their several degrees and variations. By touch I perceive hard and soft, heat and cold, motion and resistance, and of all these more and less either as to quantity or degree. Smelling furnishes me with odors; the palate with tastes; and hearing conveys sounds to the mind in all their variety of tone and composition. And as several of these are observed to accompany each other, they come to be marked by one name, and so to be reputed as one thing. Thus, for example, a certain color, taste, smell, figure and consistence having been observed to go together, are accounted one distinct thing, signified by the name APPLE. Other collections of ideas constitute a stone, a tree, a book, and the like sensible things, which as they are pleasing or disagreeable excite the passions of love, hatred, joy, grief, and so forth.

2. MIND--SPIRIT--SOUL. But, besides all that endless variety of ideas or objects of knowledge, there is likewise something which knows or perceives them, and exercises diverse operations as willing, imagining, and remembering about them. This perceiving, active being is what I call MIND, SPIRIT, SOUL, or MYSELF, by which words I do not denote any one of my ideas, but a thing entirely distinct from them, WHEREIN THEY EXIST, or, which is the same thing, whereby they are perceived—for the existence of an idea consists in being perceived.

3. HOW FAR THE ASSENT OF THE VULGAR CONCEDED. That neither our thoughts, nor passions, nor ideas formed by the imagination, exist WITHOUT the mind, is what EVERYBODY WILL ALLOW. And it seems no less evident that the various sensations or ideas imprinted on the sense, however blended or combined together (that is, whatever objects they compose), cannot exist otherwise than IN a mind perceiving them. I think an intuitive knowledge may be obtained of this by any one that shall attend to WHAT IS MEANT BY THE TERM "EXIST," when applied to sensible things. The table I write on I say exists— that is, I see and feel it—and if I were out of my study I should say it existed, meaning thereby that if I were in my study I might perceive it, or that some other spirit actually does perceive it. There was an odor, that is, it was smelt; there was a sound, that is, it was heard; a color or figure, and it was perceived by sight or touch. This is all that I can understand by these and the like expressions. For as to what is said of the absolute existence of unthinking things without any relation to their being perceived, that seems perfectly unintelligible. Their ESSE is PERCIPI, nor is it possible they should have any existence out of the minds or thinking things which perceive them.

4. THE VULGAR OPINION INVOLVES A CONTRADICTION. It is indeed an opinion STRANGELY prevailing amongst men, that houses, mountains, rivers, and in a word all sensible objects, have an existence, natural or real, distinct from their being perceived by the understanding. But, with how great an assurance and acquiescence soever this principle may be entertained in the world, yet whoever shall find in his heart to call it in question may, if I mistake not, perceive it to involve a manifest contradiction. For, what are the fore-mentioned objects but the things we perceive by sense? And what do we PERCEIVE BESIDES OUR OWN IDEAS OR SENSATIONS? And is it not plainly repugnant that any one of these, or any combination of them, should exist unperceived?

5. CAUSE OF THIS PREVALENT ERROR. If we thoroughly examine this tenet it will, perhaps, be found at bottom to depend on the doctrine of ABSTRACT IDEAS. For can there be a nicer strain of abstraction than to distinguish the existence of sensible objects from their being perceived, so as to conceive them existing unperceived? Light and colors, heat and cold, extension and figures—in a word, the things we see and feel—what are they but so many sensations, notions, ideas, or impressions on the sense? And is it possible to separate, even in thought, any of these from perception? For my part, I might as easily divide a thing from itself. I may, indeed, divide in my thoughts, or conceive apart from each other, those things which, perhaps, I never perceived by sense so divided. Thus, I imagine the trunk of a human body without the limbs, or conceive the smell of a rose without thinking on the rose itself. So far, I will not deny, I can abstract—if that may properly be called ABSTRACTION which extends only to the conceiving separately such objects as it is possible may really exist or be actually perceived asunder. But my conceiving or imagining power does not extend

beyond the possibility of real existence or perception. Hence, as it is impossible for me to see or feel anything without an actual sensation of that thing, so is it impossible for me to conceive in my thoughts any sensible thing or object distinct from the sensation or perception of it.

**Questions:**

7. Given the author's account of imagining of the smell of a rose, which one of the following is most analogous to the author's ideas in action?

    A. A man who has been alone for his whole life dreams of a woman.
    B. A bird knows how to fly south in autumn without ever having done so.
    C. A dog chases a rabbit and later dreams of a rabbit chasing him.
    D. Until a man sees another man with power and then dreams of a god, that god does not exist.
    E. A man has to see a chair without legs before he can imagine it.

8. The author of the passage would be most likely to disagree with which of the following statements?

    A. Everything exists independently of mankind.
    B. The self is synonymous with the mind.
    C. Certain things are a conglomeration of specific perception.
    D. Without considerable perception, we cannot reach complicated abstract thought.
    E. Smell is akin to taste.

9. What is the primary function of the passage's final paragraph?

    A. To function as a break from the initial argument
    B. To draw on the third and fourth paragraphs and attempt to pinpoint the source of the problem they deal with
    C. To conclude the author's argument
    D. To discuss a criticism of the argument presented by the author in the third and fourth paragraphs
    E. To discuss the abstract at a level of detail not afforded to it in the other paragraphs.

10. Which of the following is an apt description of the author's assessment of emotions in the passage?

    A. Simply spurious
    B. Extremely complex
    C. Extensive
    D. Brief and lacking detail
    E. Off-topic

11. The underlined phrase "Their ESSE is PERCIPI" as used in the third paragraph most nearly means what?

    A. Their saying is perceiving.
    B. Their attempt is acknowledged.
    C. To see them is to believe in them.
    D. Their essence is production.
    E. Their being is perception.


12. Which one of the following best captures the author's attitude toward abstract thoughts?

    A. They exist only when we put effort into perceiving them.
    B. They are not real.
    C. They are always founded on real perceptions.
    D. They are contradictory to human knowledge.
    E. They are more important than when we perceive senses.


13. Which one of the following most accurately states the main point of the passage?

    A. We perceive things with our senses then assess or transform these perceptions.
    B. Human thinking is mostly sensing things and only sometimes assessing them.
    C. None of these answers accurately convey the main point of the passage.
    D. Men are meant to dream and derive fanciful thoughts from their experienced sensations.
    E. The process of thought does not allow things to exist when we are not near them.


## Verbal Reasoning: Text Completion Task Simulation


1 - The professor's lecture on climate change was both _____ and enlightening; it not only provided the students with extensive data but also explained the implications of global warming in layman's terms.

A) convoluted
B) insightful
C) superficial

2 - Despite the CEO's efforts to revitalize the company's flagging fortunes, the initiatives were largely _____, failing to address the fundamental issues plaguing the organization.

A) innovative
B) successful

C) ineffectual

3 - The policy's _____ reception among the public was unexpected by the lawmakers, who had anticipated widespread approval and minimal opposition.

A) mixed
B) warm
C) negligible

4 - In his latest novel, the author explores themes of redemption and guilt with a _____ that resonates deeply with his readers, making it perhaps his most compelling work to date.

A) frivolity
B) sincerity
C) ambiguity

5 - While the film was criticized for its _____, its stunning visuals and innovative special effects were highly praised, drawing audiences despite poor reviews.

A) length
B) originality
C) predictability

6 - Environmental advocates argue that without a significant shift in public policy towards sustainable practices, efforts to combat climate change will be largely _____.

A) efficacious
B) redundant
C) futile

7 - The researcher's hypothesis, initially regarded as _____, gained credibility after experiments confirmed her predictions about the chemical reaction.

A) unorthodox
B) proven
C) expected

8 - His penchant for _____ solutions to routine problems ensures that his contributions to team meetings are both refreshing and highly valued by his colleagues.

A) orthodox
B) innovative
C) conventional

9 - The budget proposal was so _____, packed with jargon and extraneous details, that few could grasp its true intent and potential impact on the community.

A) streamlined

B) opaque

C) explicit

## Verbal Reasoning: Sentence Equivalence Task Simulation

1 - The city's continuous expansion is starting to have a(n) _____ effect on the surrounding rural areas, gradually integrating them into the urban landscape.

A) transformative
B) negligible
C) minimal
D) profound
E) superficial
F) revolutionary

2 - The novel's plot was _____ by critics, who found it overly complex and difficult to follow, though it was praised for its imaginative storytelling.

A) derided
B) celebrated
C) criticized
D) acclaimed
E) dismissed
F) commended

3 - Her speech was so _____ that it resonated deeply with the audience, leaving many moved and inspired by her words.

A) impactful
B) inconsequential
C) profound
D) trivial
E) affecting
F) indifferent

4 - Despite the project's ambitious scope, the team's approach has been surprisingly _____, focusing on small, manageable tasks.

A) pragmatic
B) erratic
C) idealistic
D) systematic
E) practical
F) visionary

5 - The critic's review of the film was _____; he managed to express disappointment without being overly harsh or dismissive.

A) vitriolic
B) diplomatic
C) caustic
D) tactful
E) scathing
F) considerate

6 - Global initiatives to reduce carbon emissions have been _____, as different countries manifest varying levels of commitment and effectiveness.

A) uneven
B) consistent
C) uniform
D) patchy
E) sporadic
F) steady

7 - The technology conference was highly _____; attendees gained insights from leading experts and engaged in networking opportunities.

A) informative
B) tedious
C) enlightening
D) dull
E) educational
F) boring

8 - His leadership style is often described as _____; he manages to guide his team through challenges without imposing strict controls.

A) authoritarian
B) dictatorial
C) flexible
D) rigid
E) adaptive
F) stringent

9 - The book's conclusion was _____, leaving readers to ponder the fate of the main characters long after finishing the last page.

A) definitive
B) ambiguous
C) clear
D) uncertain

E) indeterminate
F) explicit


## Quantitative Reasoning: Quantitative Comparisons Task Simulation

Quantity A: The area of a rectangle with a length 8 cm and a width of 6 cm.
Quantity B: The area of a triangle with a base 8 cm and a height of 9 cm.

Quantity A: $x$, where $x$ is the smallest prime number greater than 25.
Quantity B: 30

Quantity A: The sum of the series 2 + 4 + 6 + ... + 20.
Quantity B: The sum of the series 3 + 6 + 9 + ... + 30.

Quantity A: The value of $2^8$.
Quantity B: The value of $4^4$

Quantity A: The number of diagonals in a polygon with 10 sides.
Quantity B: 35

Quantity A: The interest earned on $1000 invested at a 5% annual compound interest rate for 2 years.
Quantity B: $100

Quantity A: The perimeter of an equilateral triangle with side length 6 cm.
Quantity B: The circumference of a circle with a radius of 3 cm (use π = 3.14).

Quantity A: The volume of a sphere with a radius of 4 cm (use $V = \frac{4}{3}\pi r^3$ for the volume of a sphere).
Quantity B: The volume of a cylinder with a radius of 4 cm and height of 4 cm (use $V = \pi r^2 h$ for the volume of a cylinder).

Quantity A: The probability of drawing a red card from a standard deck of 52 playing cards.
Quantity B: The probability of drawing a face card from the same deck.


## Quantitative Reasoning: Problem solving Task Simulation

1 - A container has 120 liters of a solution that is 30% salt. How many liters of pure water must be added to make the solution 20% salt?

2 - If x and y are positive integers such that $x^2y = 72$, what is the smallest possible value of x+y?

3 - An art dealer sells two paintings for $1500 each. On one, he makes a 20% profit and on the other, he suffers a 20% loss. What is his total profit or loss percentage on the two paintings combined?

4 - A circle is inscribed in a square. If the area of the square is 144 square units, what is the area of the circle?

5 - If the price of an item is first decreased by 30% and then increased by 30%, what is the net percent change in the price?

6 - A train 150 meters long passes a station platform in 18 seconds. If the platform is twice the length of the train, what is the speed of the train in km/h?

7 - The sum of three consecutive even numbers is 90. What is the largest number?

8 - In a certain game, scoring a "5" triples your current score, while scoring a "3" adds 20 points to your score. If a player starts with 10 points and scores two "5s" and one "3", what is their final score?

9 - A right triangle has legs of lengths 6 cm and 8 cm. What is the area of the circle circumscribed around the triangle?

10 - If 40% of a number is 80, what is 30% of that number?

11 - A clock shows the time as 3:15 PM. What is the angle between the hour and the minute hands?

12 - A population of bacteria doubles every 20 minutes. If the population is initially 1000, what will it be in one hour?

13 - If five times the fifth term of an arithmetic sequence is equal to three times the ninth term, what is the first term if the common difference is 2?

# Quantitative Reasoning: Data Interpretation Task Simulation

1 - Graph Type: Line Graph

Data Content: Quarterly profits over two years for Companies A and B.

Question: Which company exhibited greater growth in Year 2 compared to Year 1?

Choices:
A) Company A
B) Company B
C) Both companies showed equal growth
D) Neither company showed growth

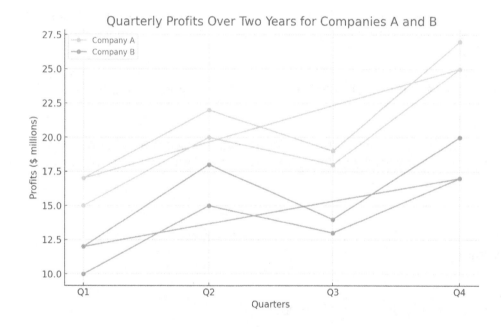

2 - Graph Type: Bar Graph

Data Content: Sales data by product category (Electronics, Apparel, Home Goods, Books) across six regions.

Question: Identify the region with the most balanced sales distribution across all product categories.

Choices:
A) North
B) South

C) Central
D) International
E) West
F) East

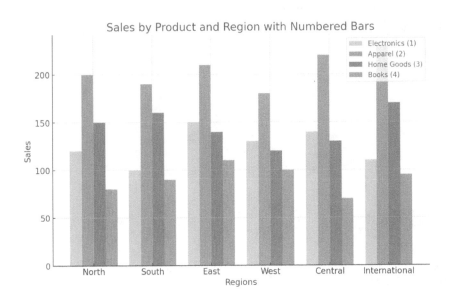

3 - Graph Type: Pie Chart

Data Content: Market shares of competitors A, B, C, D, E.

Question: What is the market value of each competitor if the total market is valued at $2 billion?

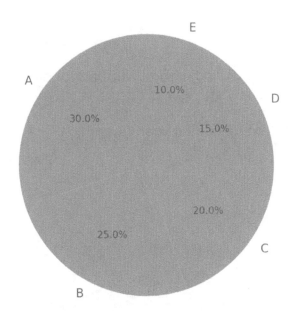

4 - Graph Type: Histogram

Data Content: Distribution of student scores across five ranges.
Question: Which score range is the median, and how many students fall within this range?

Choices:
A) 0-20
B) 21-40
C) 41-60
D) 61-80

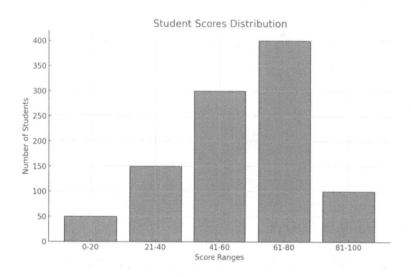

5 - Graph Type: Stacked Column Chart

Data Content: Monthly energy consumption by source (Solar, Wind, Hydro, Nuclear) for one year.

Question: How does the total energy consumption vary throughout the year, and which energy source is the highest contributor in December?

Choices:
A) Solar
B) Wind
C) Hydro
D) Nuclear

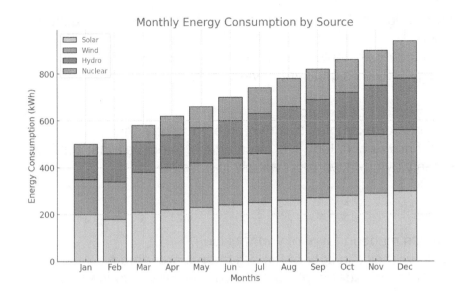

# Answer Sheet

## Analytical Writing: Issue Task Simulation

"Technology ultimately separates and alienates people more than it serves to bring them together."

**Essay Planning Guide**

**Introduction**:

Thesis Statement: Clearly state whether you agree or disagree with the prompt. Provide a brief rationale for your position.
Example: "While technology can indeed lead to a sense of isolation among individuals, its capabilities for connecting people across vast distances fundamentally outweigh these concerns."

**Body Paragraphs**:

Paragraph 1: Argument Supporting Your Thesis
Main Idea: Provide a compelling argument that supports your thesis.
Example: Discuss how technology enables real-time communication and fosters relationships across different geographical locations.

Paragraph 2: Counterargument and Rebuttal
Main Idea: Address a potential counterargument to show depth of thought.

Counterargument Example: Acknowledge that technology can lead to superficial interactions or diminish face-to-face engagement.
Rebuttal Example: Argue that the benefits of increased access to information and social support networks through technology provide significant advantages.

Paragraph 3: Further Supporting Argument or Example
Main Idea: Provide additional evidence or examples that reinforce your main thesis.
Example: Illustrate with examples of how technology has been crucial in educational contexts, connecting students and teachers in ways that were previously impossible.

**Conclusion**:

Summary: Recap the main arguments made in favor of your position.
Restatement of Thesis: Reinforce your thesis in light of the arguments presented.
Closing Thought: Offer a final thought or broader implication of your argument to leave a strong impression.
Example: "Ultimately, technology acts as a bridge rather than a barrier, uniting people across the myriad divides of the modern world."

**Evaluation Criteria** (For Review and Self-Assessment)
Clarity and Precision: How clear and precise was the articulation of ideas?
Coherence and Logic: How well did the essay flow? Were the transitions logical?
Relevance and Support: Were the examples and arguments relevant and well-supported?
Syntax and Grammar: How proficient was the use of language and grammar?

This structured guide serves as an "answer sheet" to help plan, write, and review your essay in response to the given Issue Prompt on the GRE. Remember, the key to a high-scoring GRE essay is a clear position, logical argumentation, and varied, precise use of language.


# Verbal Reasoning: Reading Comprehension Task Simulation

1. **Correct Answer:** Create a system of incentives for countries to fight human trafficking, while also tracking which countries are effectively addressing the issue

**Explanation:** The best answer will cover the two primary purposes behind the TIPS report: to instill change in how countries address the issue of human trafficking, and to also document the issue more effectively. The correct answer choice mentions both of these priorities:
Create a system of incentives for countries to fight human trafficking, while also tracking which countries are effectively addressing the issue


2. **Correct Answer:** Show how the United States ranks countries' efforts to combat human trafficking

**Explanation:** The tier system is described in order to explain how the United States categorizes different countries according to how they address the issue of human trafficking. Therefore, the correct answer is:
Show how the United States ranks countries' efforts to combat human trafficking
A tempting incorrect answer is: Simplify a complex problem. This is incorrect because while the tier system might have this effect, that was not the author's intended message when describing the tier system.


3. **Correct Answer:** Describe a type of report produced by the United States

**Explanation:** The entire focus of the text is on the TIPS Report and how it is formulated. Therefore, the best answer is:
Describe a type of report produced by the United States
The incorrect answers are either too broad or only apply to certain parts of the text, rather than the text as a whole.


4. **Correct Answer:** Objectively descriptive of how the TIPS Report is used to assess countries' actions against human trafficking

**Explanation:** The tone is very objective and descriptive; its intent is simply to communicate information, not to inspire admiration, enthusiasm, or emotion. Additionally, the text is not disinterested. Therefore, the correct answer is:
Objectively descriptive of how the TIPS Report is used to assess countries' actions against human trafficking


5. **Correct Answer:** Being punished by the World Bank

**Explanation:** While one of the potential consequences of being a Tier 3 country is that the U.S. may pressure the World Bank to limit assistance, the World Bank would not itself punish a Tier 3 country of its own accord. Therefore, the correct answer is:
Being punished by the World Bank


6. **Correct Answer:** To suggest that the TIPS Report is politically biased

**Explanation:** The author mentions that U.S. missions regularly meet with foreign officials in order to cast the TIPS Report in a positive light, to show a willingness on part of the U.S. to engage in a dialogue and cooperate with other countries, and to offer insight as to how data is collected. The only answer choice that does not reflect this mission is:
To suggest that the TIPS Report is politically biased.


7. **Correct Answer:** A dog chases a rabbit and later dreams of a rabbit chasing him.

**Explanation:** The specific instance of the rose, which comes in the last paragraph, is this: "I imagine the trunk of a human body without the limbs, or conceive the smell of a rose without thinking on the rose itself." The author's ideas here are that we cannot change something in our minds until we have perceived it. The dog has perceived chasing the rabbit and is therefore following the author's ideas when it dreams that the role between it and the rabbit are changed. At least two of the other answers go against the author's ideas in that no perception occurs. The other two are not analogous to the image of the rose's scent and perhaps go beyond the author's overall argument.

8. **Correct Answer:** Everything exists independently of mankind.

**Explanation:** It is quite obvious that the statement "Everything exists independently of mankind" is the one argument with which the author would be most likely to disagree. Despite the fact that the author makes no distinction between the thoughts of humans and other living things, we can assume that he is talking with specific reference to humanity. If humans did not exist, then in the author's opinion everything else's existence would perhaps be invalid. If you were to ask the author the famous riddle, "If a tree falls in the woods and no one is around to hear it, does it make a sound?" he would be quite adamant in answering "no."

9. **Correct Answer:** To draw on the third and fourth paragraphs and attempt to pinpoint the source of the problem they deal with

**Explanation:** We can tell from the paragraphs' clear titles that the author intended to have the fifth paragraph pinpoint the problem discussed in the third and fourth paragraphs. In order, they are titled, "HOW FAR THE ASSENT OF THE VULGAR CONCEDED," "THE VULGAR OPINION INVOLVES A CONTRADICTION," and "CAUSE OF THIS PREVALENT ERROR." The author does in part detail the abstract in this paragraph, but it is not the paragraph's primary function.

10. **Correct Answer:** Brief and lacking detail

**Explanation:** The author does not fully address emotions in the passage; he only mentions emotions when he says at the end of the first paragraph, "Other collections of ideas constitute a stone, a tree, a book, and the like sensible things, which as they are pleasing or disagreeable excite the passions of love, hatred, joy, grief, and so forth." In relation to the rest of the passage, this is perhaps the briefest address of any subject mentioned. The use of the phrase
"and so forth" emphasizes how brief the assessment of emotions is, as if they may undermine his argument.

11. **Correct Answer:** Their being is perception.

**Explanation:** The saying "ESSE is PERCIPI" means "to be is to be perceived," and we can interpret this despite it being in a different language. We can either spend time discovering the links between the words

"esse" and "essence" and "percipi" and "perceived," or we can use the author's argument in the preceding sentence to guide us in the right direction: "nor is it possible they should have any existence out of the minds or thinking things which perceive them." Be careful here to read the answers carefully as many of their words look similar but have vastly different meanings.

12. **Correct Answer:** They are always founded on real perceptions.

**Explanation:** If we look at the last paragraph, which is largely about abstract thoughts, we can see that the author says "my conceiving or imagining power does not extend beyond the possibility of real existence or perception." Abstract thoughts are thus founded in reality according to the author. We could perhaps say that "they exist only when we put effort into perceiving them," however, the author never says this outright.

13. **Correct Answer:** We perceive things with our senses then assess or transform these perceptions.

**Explanation:** The passage quite clearly states at the beginning that we perceive things, then other parts which may be called "mind, body, or spirit" [exercise] diverse operations as willing, imagining, and remembering about them." We can say this continues on to the end of the passage as the author discusses in more detail the

"imagining" portion of our perceptions. We cannot say that the statement "Human thinking is mostly sensing things and only sometimes assessing them" is correct, as the word "sometimes" nullifies it. Likewise, the statement "The process of thought does not allow things to exist when we are not near them" is nullified by being a simplified, perhaps inaccurate, argument of a part of the passage, not of the whole passage.


# Verbal Reasoning: Text Completion Task Simulation


1 - The professor's lecture on climate change was both _____ and enlightening; it not only provided the students with extensive data but also explained the implications of global warming in layman's terms.

**Answer:** B) insightful

**Explanation:** The use of "enlightening" suggests that the lecture provided a deep understanding, making "insightful" the correct choice as it complements the context of providing clarity and depth of knowledge.

2 - Despite the CEO's efforts to revitalize the company's flagging fortunes, the initiatives were largely _____, failing to address the fundamental issues plaguing the organization.

**Answer**: C) ineffectual

**Explanation**: The phrase "failing to address the fundamental issues" implies that the initiatives did not achieve their intended effect, making "ineffectual" the appropriate choice.

3 - The policy's _____ reception among the public was unexpected by the lawmakers, who had anticipated widespread approval and minimal opposition.

**Answer**: A) mixed

**Explanation**: The lawmakers' surprise at the reception suggests it was neither fully positive nor fully negative, hence "mixed" fits best, indicating a reception that included both support and opposition.

4 - In his latest novel, the author explores themes of redemption and guilt with a _____ that resonates deeply with his readers, making it perhaps his most compelling work to date.

**Answer**: B) sincerity

**Explanation**: The depth of resonance with readers about serious themes like redemption and guilt suggests a genuine and earnest exploration, which is captured by "sincerity."

5 - While the film was criticized for its _____, its stunning visuals and innovative special effects were highly praised, drawing audiences despite poor reviews.

**Answer**: C) predictability

**Explanation**: The contrast set up by the sentence between criticism and praise suggests the missing word is a negative attribute, making "predictability" the best fit, as it is a common criticism that does not affect visual appeal.

6 - Environmental advocates argue that without a significant shift in public policy towards sustainable practices, efforts to combat climate change will be largely _____.

**Answer**: C) futile
**Explanation**: The context implies that without change, efforts will be ineffective, which is best described by "futile," meaning incapable of producing any useful result.

7 - The researcher's hypothesis, initially regarded as _____, gained credibility after experiments confirmed her predictions about the chemical reaction.

**Answer**: A) unorthodox

**Explanation**: The term "unorthodox" suggests that the hypothesis was unconventional or out of the mainstream, aligning with the idea that it was not initially accepted but later validated by experimental results.

8 - His penchant for _____ solutions to routine problems ensures that his contributions to team meetings are both refreshing and highly valued by his colleagues.

**Answer**: B) innovative

**Explanation**: The clues "refreshing" and "highly valued" suggest that his solutions are creative and effective, making "innovative" the appropriate choice as it implies introducing new and creative ideas.

9 - The budget proposal was so _____, packed with jargon and extraneous details, that few could grasp its true intent and potential impact on the community.

**Answer**: B) opaque

**Explanation**: The description of the proposal as packed with jargon and hard to understand suggests "opaque" as the fitting choice, meaning not easy to see through or understand.

## Verbal Reasoning: Sentence Equivalence Task Simulation

1 - The city's continuous expansion is starting to have a(n) _____ effect on the surrounding rural areas, gradually integrating them into the urban landscape.

**Answers**: A) transformative, F) revolutionary

**Explanation**: Both "transformative" and "revolutionary" imply significant and thorough changes, fitting the context of the city's expansion affecting rural areas deeply.

2 - The novel's plot was _____ by critics, who found it overly complex and difficult to follow, though it was praised for its imaginative storytelling.

**Answers**: A) derided, C) criticized

**Explanation**: "Derided" and "criticized" both imply negative feedback, aligning with the critics' view of the plot as overly complex.

3 - Her speech was so _____ that it resonated deeply with the audience, leaving many moved and inspired by her words.

**Answers**: A) impactful, C) profound

**Explanation**: "Impactful" and "profound" both denote a deep, significant effect, suitable for describing a speech that resonated strongly with the audience.

4 - Despite the project's ambitious scope, the team's approach has been surprisingly _____, focusing on small, manageable tasks.

**Answers**: A) pragmatic, E) practical

**Explanation**: Both "pragmatic" and "practical" suggest a realistic and sensible approach, fitting the context of focusing on manageable tasks despite the ambitious nature of the project.

5 - The critic's review of the film was _____; he managed to express disappointment without being overly harsh or dismissive.

**Answers**: B) diplomatic, D) tactful

**Explanation**: "Diplomatic" and "tactful" both imply careful and sensitive communication, especially suitable for expressing criticism without being harsh.

6 - Global initiatives to reduce carbon emissions have been _____, as different countries manifest varying levels of commitment and effectiveness.

**Answers**: A) uneven, D) patchy

**Explanation**: Both "uneven" and "patchy" describe something that is not consistent or uniform, matching the description of varied commitment levels across countries.

7 - The technology conference was highly _____; attendees gained insights from leading experts and engaged in networking opportunities.

**Answers**: A) informative, C) enlightening

**Explanation**: "Informative" and "enlightening" both describe experiences that provide significant knowledge or insight, fitting a conference that offered valuable information and learning opportunities.

8 - His leadership style is often described as _____; he manages to guide his team through challenges without imposing strict controls.

**Answers**: C) flexible, E) adaptive

**Explanation**: Both "flexible" and "adaptive" indicate an ability to adjust or modify approaches as needed, suitable for a leadership style that is accommodating rather than rigid.

9 - The book's conclusion was _____, leaving readers to ponder the fate of the main characters long after finishing the last page.

**Answers**: B) ambiguous, E) indeterminate

**Explanation**: "Ambiguous" and "indeterminate" both refer to situations that are not clearly defined or decided, perfectly describing a conclusion that leaves much open to the reader's interpretation.


## Quantitative Reasoning: Quantitative Comparisons Task Simulation


Quantity A: The area of a rectangle with length 8 cm and width 6 cm (Area = 48 cm²).
Quantity B: The area of a triangle with base 8 cm and height 9 cm (Area = 0.5 * 8 * 9 = 36 cm²).

**Answer**: Quantity A is greater.

**Explanation**: The area of the rectangle (48 cm²) is greater than that of the triangle (36 cm²).

Quantity A: $x$ is the smallest prime number greater than 25 (29).
Quantity B: 30

**Answer**: Quantity B is greater.

**Explanation**: The smallest prime number greater than 25 is 29, which is less than 30.

Quantity A: The sum of the series 2 + 4 + 6 + ... + 20 (110).
Quantity B: The sum of the series 3 + 6 + 9 + ... + 30 (165).

**Answer:** Quantity B is greater.

**Explanation**: The sum of the arithmetic series from 2 to 20 (increasing by 2) is 110, while the sum from 3 to 30 (increasing by 3) is 165.

Quantity A: The value of $2^8$.
Quantity B: The value of $4^4$

**Answer**: The quantities are equal.

**Explanation**: Both expressions evaluate to 256.

Quantity A: The number of diagonals in a polygon with 10 sides (35).
Quantity B: 35

**Answer**: The quantities are equal.

**Explanation**: A polygon with 10 sides has $\frac{10(10-3)}{2} = 35$ diagonals.

Quantity A: The interest earned on $1000 at 5% annual compound interest for 2 years (approximately $102.50).
Quantity B: $100

**Answer**: Quantity A is greater.

**Explanation**: The compound interest for two years is slightly more than $100 ($102.50), calculated using the formula $P(1 + r)^n - P$ where $P = 1000$, $r = 0.05$, and $n = 2$.


Quantity A: The perimeter of an equilateral triangle with side length 6 cm (18 cm).
Quantity B: The circumference of a circle with a radius of 3 cm (approximately 18.84 cm).

**Answer**: Quantity B is greater.

**Explanation**: The perimeter of the triangle is 18 cm, while the circumference of the circle, calculated as $2\pi r$, is approximately 18.84 cm.

Quantity A: The volume of a sphere with radius 4 cm ( $\frac{256}{3} \pi \approx 268.08$ cm³).
Quantity B: The volume of a cylinder with radius 4 cm and height 4 cm ($64\pi r \approx 201.06$ cm³).

**Answer**: Quantity A is greater.

**Explanation**: The volume of the sphere is greater than the volume of the cylinder, calculated using the given formulas.

Quantity A: The probability of drawing a red card from a standard deck of 52 playing cards ( $\frac{1}{2}$ ).
Quantity B: The probability of drawing a face card from the same deck ( $\frac{3}{13}$ ).

**Answer**: Quantity A is greater.

**Explanation**: There are 26 red cards in a deck, so the probability of drawing one is $\frac{1}{2}$, which is greater than the probability of drawing one of the 12 face cards, $\frac{3}{13}$ .


## Quantitative Reasoning: Problem solving Task Simulation


1 - To reduce the concentration of salt from 30% to 20%, calculate the additional water required:

144

**Explanation**: Let $x$ be the liters of water added. The new solution volume will be $120 + x$. The salt remains 36 liters. Setting up the equation: $\frac{36}{120+x} = 0.2$. Solving this, $x = 60$ liters.

**Answer**: 60 liters of water must be added.


2 - Finding the smallest possible value of $x + y$ given $x^2y = 72$:

**Explanation**: Factorizing 72, we consider $x = 6$ and $y = 2$ (since $6^2 \times 2 = 72$). This gives the smallest sum $x + y = 8$.

**Answer**: The smallest possible value of $x + y$ is 8.


3 - Calculating the overall profit or loss from selling two paintings:

**Explanation**: Selling each for $1500, one at a 20% profit means purchase at $1250; one at a 20% loss means purchase at $1875. Total spent is $3125 and total received is $3000, leading to a loss. The percentage loss is $\frac{125}{3125} \times 100 = 4\%$.

**Answer**: Overall, he has a 4% loss.


4 - Finding the area of a circle inscribed in a square with area 144 square units:

**Explanation**: Side length of the square = $\sqrt{144}$ =12 units. Radius of the circle is half that, 6 units. Area of the circle = $\pi \times 6^2$ =36π square units.

**Answer**: The area of the circle is 36π square units.


5 - Net percent change in the price after decreasing and then increasing by 30%:

**Explanation**: Let initial price be $P$. Final price after changes = $P \times 0.7 \times 1.3 = 0.91P$. Net change = −9%.

**Answer:** The net percent change in the price is a decrease of 9%.


6 - Determining the speed of a train passing a platform:

**Explanation**: Total distance = length of train + length of platform = 150 + 300 = 450 meters. Speed = $\frac{450}{18}$ m/s = 25 m/s or $25 \times \frac{3600}{1000}$ km/h = 90 km/h.

**Answer**: The speed of the train is 90 km/h.

7 - Finding the largest of three consecutive even numbers summing to 90:

**Explanation**: Let the numbers be $x$, $x+2$, $x+4$. Then $3x + 6 = 90$, solving for $x$ gives $x = 28$. The largest number is $x + 4 = 32$.

**Answer:** The largest number is 32.


8 - Calculating final score in a game starting with 10 points:

**Explanation**: First 5 triples it to 30, second 5 triples again to 90, and a 3 adds 20 making it 110.

**Answer**: The final score is 110.


9 - Area of the circumscribed circle around a right triangle:

**Explanation**: Hypotenuse is 10 cm (right triangle with 6 and 8 cm sides), radius of the circumcircle R = $\frac{hypotenuse}{2}$ = 5 cm. Area = π × R² = 25π square cm.

**Answer**: Area is 25π square cm.


10 - Calculating 30% of a number when 40% is 80:

**Explanation**: If 40% is 80, 100% is 200. Thus, 30% of 200 is 60.

**Answer**: 30% of the number is 60.


11 - Angle between the hour and minute hands at 3:15 PM:

**Explanation**: At 3:15, the minute hand is at 90 degrees (15 minutes), and the hour hand is at 97.5 degrees (3 hours + 15 minutes). The angle between them is | 97.5 − 90 | = 7.5 degrees.

**Answer**: The angle is 7.5 degrees.


12 - Population of bacteria doubling every 20 minutes, starting at 1000:

**Explanation**: After one hour (3 doublings), the population is 1000 × 2³ = 8000.

**Answer**: The population after one hour is 8000.

13 - Finding the first term of an arithmetic sequence given conditions on terms:

**Explanation**: If $5a_5 = 3a_9$ , substituting $a_n = a + (n - 1)d$ (where $d = 2$), we solve for $a$. This yields $a = 4$.

**Answer**: The first term is 4.

## Quantitative Reasoning: Data Interpretation Task Simulation

1 - Profit Growth Analysis:

Company A:
Year 1 Total: 15+20+18+25=78 million dollars
Year 2 Total: 17+22+19+27=85 million dollars
Growth from Year 1 to Year 2: 85−78=7 million dollars

Company B:
Year 1 Total: 10+15+13+17=55 million dollars
Year 2 Total: 12+18+14+20=64 million dollars
Growth from Year 1 to Year 2: 64−55=9 million dollars

From this analysis, Company B showed greater growth in Year 2 compared to Year 1, with an increase of 9 million dollars over Company A's growth of 7 million dollars. Therefore, Company B demonstrated a stronger upward trend in profits during the second year.

**The correct answer is**: B) Company B

2 - From the analysis of the standard deviation of sales across product categories within each region, the West region has the lowest standard deviation at approximately 29.47. This lower value indicates that the West region exhibits the most balanced sales distribution across all product categories compared to the other regions.

Thus, the correct answer to the exam question about which region shows the most balanced sales across all product categories is West. This region demonstrated the smallest variability in sales figures across the different categories, indicating a more uniform distribution of sales performance
**The correct answer is**: E) West

3 - From the calculations:

Competitor A controls 30% of the market, which translates to a market value of $600 million. Competitor B controls 25% of the market, equating to $500 million.

Competitor C controls 20% of the market, resulting in $400 million.
Competitor D controls 15% of the market, corresponding to $300 million.
Competitor E controls 10% of the market, leading to $200 million.

These figures provide the exact market value for each competitor based on the given total market worth. This visualization helps clarify the proportionate influence of each competitor within the market

4 - From the analysis, the median score range is determined by finding the range where the cumulative number of students reaches the halfway point of the total student count. Given the data:

The total number of students is 1000.
The cumulative count reaches 500 (the median position) within the score range 41-60.
Thus, the median score range is 41-60, with 300 students falling into this category. This range represents the middle of the distribution in terms of student scores, indicating that half of the students scored below 60 and half scored above 41.

**The correct answer is**: C) 41-60

5 - Analysis:

Trend Over the Year:
The total energy consumption steadily increases over the year. The graph shows a clear upward trend from January to December, indicating higher energy production and/or usage as the year progresses.

Contribution in December:
In December, the energy source that contributes the most is Solar, with 300 kWh. This is visually evident as the top segment in the December column, which is the largest among all the energy sources for that month.

**The correct answer is**: A) Solar

# Practice Test 9: Complete Simulation

**Analytical Writing: Issue Task Simulation**

## Instructions

You will be given a statement about a general interest topic. Your task is to write a well-organized essay in which you explain the extent to which you agree or disagree with the statement and support your viewpoint with reasons and examples.

**Time allowed:** 30 minutes

## Issue Prompt

"The expansion of global trade has improved the standard of living in developing nations at the expense of economic stability and equitable growth in developed countries."

## Task

Write a response in which you discuss the extent to which you agree or disagree with the statement above. In developing and supporting your position, you should consider ways in which the statement might or might not hold true and explain how these considerations shape your position.

## Points to Consider

1. **Impact on developing nations:** Evaluate the extent to which global trade has facilitated economic growth in developing nations. Has it provided improved access to goods, services, and employment opportunities that uplift communities, or has it deepened inequalities and reinforced existing disparities?
2. **Effects on developed countries:** Assess the impact of global trade on developed nations. Has it led to the offshoring of jobs, deindustrialization, and economic insecurity for certain sectors, or has it created new opportunities for innovation and growth in other industries?
3. **Income inequality:** Analyze how global trade affects income inequality both within and between nations. Has it widened the gap between rich and poor, or has it contributed to a more equitable distribution of wealth and opportunity?
4. **Economic stability:** Consider the impact of global trade on economic stability. Has it led to greater economic interconnectedness and stability, or has it exposed countries to greater volatility and risk due to global economic fluctuations?

## Writing Tips

**Introduction:** Clearly introduce your viewpoint on the issue. State whether you agree or disagree with the prompt, and summarize the main reasons for your position.

**Body paragraphs:** Each paragraph should focus on a specific reason or example supporting your viewpoint. Use clear topic sentences, and provide concrete examples or data where possible.

**Counterarguments:** Consider acknowledging a counterargument to show that you have thought about the issue from multiple perspectives. Explain why this counterargument does not change your overall position.

**Conclusion:** Summarize your argument and reinforce how the examples you provided support your viewpoint.


## Verbal Reasoning: Reading Comprehension Task Simulation

**Passage:**

We cannot inquire far into the meaning of proverbs or traditional sayings without discovering that the common understanding of general and abstract names is loose and uncertain. Common speech is a quicksand.

Consider how we acquire our vocabulary, how we pick up the words that we use from our neighbors and from books, and why this is so soon becomes apparent. Theoretically, we know the full meaning of a name when we know all the attributes that it connotes, and we are not justified in extending it except to objects that possess all the attributes. This is the logical ideal, but between the ought to be of Logic and the is of practical life, there is a vast difference. How seldom do we conceive words in their full meaning! And who is to instruct us in the full meaning? It is not as in the exact sciences, where we start with knowledge of the full meaning. In Geometry, for example, we learn the definitions of the words used, "point," "line," "parallel," etc., before we proceed to use them. But in common speech, we hear the words applied to individual objects; we utter them in the same connection; we extend them to other objects that strike us as like without knowing the precise points of likeness that the convention of common speech includes. The more exact meaning we learn by gradual induction from individual cases. The individual's extension of the name proceeds upon what in the objects has most impressed him when he caught the word: this may differ in different individuals; the usage of neighbors corrects individual eccentricities. The child in arms shouts "Da" at the passing stranger who reminds him of his father; for him at first it is a general name applicable to every man; by degrees he learns that for him it is a singular name.

It is obvious that to avoid error and confusion, the meaning or connotation of names, the concepts, should somehow be fixed; names cannot otherwise have an identical reference in human intercourse. We may call this ideal fixed concept the Logical Concept. But in actual speech we have also the Personal Concept, which varies more or less with the individual user, and the Popular or Vernacular Concept, which, though roughly fixed, varies from social sect to social sect and from generation to generation.

When we come to words of which the logical concept is a complex relation, an obscure or intangible attribute, the defects of the popular conception and its tendencies to change and confusion are of the greatest practical importance. Take such words as "monarchy," "civil freedom," "landlord," "culture." Not merely should we find it difficult to give an analytic definition of such words; we might be unable to do so, and yet flatter ourselves that we had a clear understanding of their meaning.

It was with reference to this state of things that Hegel formulated his paradox that the true abstract thinker is the plain man who laughs at philosophy as what he calls abstract and unpractical. He holds decided opinions for or against this or the other abstraction, "freedom," "tyranny," "revolution," "reform," "socialism," but what these words mean and within what limits the things signified are desirable or undesirable, he is in too great a hurry to pause and consider.

The disadvantages of this kind of "abstract" thinking are obvious. The accumulated wisdom of mankind is stored in language. Until we have cleared our conceptions, and penetrated to the full meaning of words, that wisdom is a sealed book to us. Wise maxims are interpreted by us hastily in accordance with our own narrow conceptions. All the vocabulary of a language may be more or less familiar to us, and yet we may not have learnt it as an instrument of thought.

**Questions:**

1. The author's tone in this passage could best be described as _____.

    A. nonchalant and withdrawn
    B. demanding and meticulous
    C. authoritative and assured
    D. pessimistic and ambivalent
    E. haughty and condescending

2. The underlined clause "Common speech is a quicksand" could be most reasonably assumed to mean which of the following?

    A. It is easy to get lost in English due to the abundance of words used to describe the same thing.
    B. The definitions of English words are being altered by academic dictates.
    C. The definition of English words and phrases are often vague and debatable.
    D. English expressions are confusing.
    E. English regional vernacular is being lost.

3. Which of these bests restates the author's meaning in the underlined selection, "It is obvious that to avoid error and confusion, the meaning or connotation of names, the concepts, should somehow be fixed: names cannot otherwise have an identical reference in human intercourse"?

    A. The meaning and connotation of names can be fixed, so that human intercourse will proceed without confusion and error.
    B. It is of fundamental importance that the meaning of words and names be understood universally by all people to prevent debate and unnecessary arguments.
    C. If words and names are to mean the same thing to all people, than the meanings and implications of those words must be somehow conclusively determined.

D. Trying to avoid error and confusion by fixing the meaning of words would eliminate the variety and beauty of the English vernacular language.

E. It is apparent that the meaning of names and words cannot be fixed in human interaction because such an undertaking is beyond the scope of any one person or institution.

4. How does the Personal Concept differ from the Vernacular Concept as defined by the author?

    A. It is impossible to say, as the author does not define what he means by the Vernacular Concept.

    B. The Personal Concept is highly unpredictable, whereas the Vernacular Concept is easy to understand.

    C. The Vernacular Concept allows for identical usage across human intercourse, whereas the Personal Concept varies by individual.

    D. The Personal Concept is rigidly defined, whereas the Vernacular Concept is loose and fluid.

    E. The Vernacular Concept varies by social group or generation, whereas the Personal Concept varies by individual.

5. Which of these bests summarizes the main point of the sixth paragraph?

    A. Hegel's "abstract" thinking is not applicable to the author's argument because it ignores the preconceptions that blind each individual to the true meaning of words and names.

    B. Our individual preconceptions blind us to the true meaning of words and prevent us from accurately penetrating the combined knowledge of humanity.

    C. None of these answers accurately summarizes the point of the sixth paragraph.

    D. In order to fix the problems associated with "abstract" thinking we must collectively focus on deep thinking and a scientific classification of words and names.

    E. We acquire words through natural means and as such the meanings and definitions of those words will always differ greatly from person to person.

6. Which of these best captures the main idea of the second paragraph?

    A. We learn the meaning of most words organically and as a result the exact definition and application of those words will differ from person to person.

    B. Babies learn words without being intentionally taught them and seem to develop incorrect assumptions about the meanings of certain words.

    C. It is impossible to define the vast majority of words because people have their own personal ideas about how each thing could best be described.

    D. People learn the meaning of words best when those words are specifically and rigidly defined.

    E. People learn words before they really understand them and if we want to have consistency in language we must teach the word and its correct meaning simultaneously.

**Passage:**

The United Nations Convention on Contracts for the International Sale of Goods (CISG) can help countries throughout the world have a more uniform way of navigating the challenging waters of international law surrounding trade. It is not uncommon for two countries to have adopted different laws on international trade that conflict with each other. This becomes a serious problem when trade disputes arise. To help make this concept more tangible, consider the following hypothetical.

Suppose China ships three million dollars' worth of electronics to Uganda using standard bulk shipping transportation methods via a commonly traveled sea route. However, the packaging isn't secured in a manner sufficient to withstand unforeseen weather conditions. As a result, the goods become damaged in transit and are no longer fit for resale. Given that two countries are involved in this transaction–China and Uganda–the question arises as to which country's trade laws will apply to resolve the matter at hand.

In this scenario, it is fortunate that both China and Uganda are parties to the CISG, which provide for a uniform set of laws governing trade. Such laws cover which party would be responsible for the damaged goods in this scenario. As a result, there will be no dispute as to whether China's or Uganda's trade laws apply. Given that both countries are parties to the CISG, the laws set forth by the CISG would be applicable.

However, not all countries are parties to the CISG. One example is Rwanda. Even though Rwanda is not a party to the CISG, the fact of the matter is that CISG laws can still apply to it. The CISG applies to trade between countries so long as one of those countries is a party to the CISG (unless the parties expressly specify that the CISG will not apply to their specific trade arrangement). Several of Rwanda's main trade partners, such as the United States, China, Belgium, and Uganda, are parties to the CISG, so the laws of the treaty will apply in those trade agreements. Meanwhile, there is a different story when it comes to Rwanda's trade agreements with Kenya, Swaziland, Tanzania, and Thailand, which are not parties to the CISG. Due to these countries' lack of membership in the CISG, if a problem ever arose in a trade agreement between Rwanda and one those countries, it would be unclear as to which country's laws would apply.

There has been <u>heated discussion</u> as to whether Rwanda should sign the CISG. The United Nations Development Program takes the stance that it would behoove Rwanda to join. Whether or not Rwanda decides to become a member, the CISG will still apply to a large portion of its trade agreements, as about 100 countries are in fact CISG members, with a strong portion of those members also being trade partners with Rwanda. On the flip side, some Rwandan politicians believe that valuable autonomy would be lost if Rwanda assented to the CISG. However, given the potential benefits that Rwanda stands to gain from the CISG, these fears do not merit forgoing such a valuable opportunity.

**Questions:**

7. Which of the following, if true, best supports the author's contention that Rwanda should become a member of the CISG?

    A. Participation fees for becoming a CISG member can hinder certain countries from joining.
    B. Status as a CISG member can deter non-CISG countries from engaging in trade arrangements.
    C. Becoming a CISG member can sometimes delay the processing of trade agreements because additional protocols are set in place for members to follow.
    D. Even if a country is a CISG member, commercial trade disputes are just as likely to occur.
    E. Disputes over which country's laws to apply in commercial trade situations can chill future trade arrangements with other countries, even those which belong to the CISG.

8. The author would most likely agree with which of these statements?

    A. It would be to Rwanda's benefit to join the CISG.
    B. The CISG has a narrow window of applicability.
    C. Although joining the CISG has benefits, Rwanda ultimately should not join the CISG.
    D. There are positive and negative aspects that Rwanda should weigh and balance when deciding whether to join the CISG.
    E. It is imperative that Rwanda join the CISG in order to avoid impending trade disputes that could prove to be disastrous.

9. The primary purpose of the second paragraph is to _____.

    A. provide an example that makes an abstract concept easier to understand
    B. demonstrate the deleterious effects that can result from a trade dispute
    C. suggest that China and Uganda should join the CISG
    D. directly support the author's thesis
    E. indirectly offer a counter-argument to the author's thesis

10. Which of the following is the main purpose of the article?

    A. To explain how the landscape of international trade has evolved in recent years
    B. To explain why Rwanda should become a member of the CISG
    C. To provide a broad overview of Rwanda's trading practices
    D. To weigh and balance the reasons why Rwanda should join the CISG versus why Rwanda should not join the CISG
    E. To argue that countries should always heed the recommendations of the United Nations Development Program

11. The use of the underlined phrase "heated discussion" in the context of the last paragraph of the passage most closely means _____.

A. combative discourse
B. unfair exchange
C. emotional conversation
D. strong debate
E. intense persuasion


**Passage:**

With the American people, and through them all others, familiarity with the buffalo has bred contempt. The incredible numbers in which the animals of this species formerly existed made their slaughter an easy matter, so much so that the hunters and frontiersmen who accomplished their destruction have handed down to us a contemptuous opinion of the size, character, and general presence of our bison. And how could it be otherwise than that a man who could find it in his heart to murder a majestic bull bison for a hide worth only a dollar should form a one-dollar estimate of the grandest ruminant that ever trod the earth? Men who butcher African elephants for the sake of their ivory also entertain a similar estimate of their victims.

By a combination of unfortunate circumstances, the American bison is destined to go down to posterity shorn of the honor which is his due, and appreciated at only half his worth. The hunters who slew him were from the very beginning so absorbed in the scramble for spoils that they had no time to measure or weigh him, nor even to notice the majesty of his personal appearance on his native heath. In captivity, he fails to develop as finely as in his wild state, and with the loss of his liberty, he becomes a tame-looking animal. He gets fat and short-bodied, and the lack of vigorous and constant exercise prevents the development of bone and muscle which made the prairie animal what he was.

From observations made upon buffaloes that have been reared in captivity, I am firmly convinced that confinement and semi-domestication are destined to effect striking changes in the form of Bison americanus. While this is to be expected to a certain extent with most large species, the changes promise to be most conspicuous in the buffalo. The most striking change is in the body between the hips and the shoulders. As before remarked, it becomes astonishingly short and rotund, and through liberal feeding and total lack of exercise, the muscles of the shoulders and hindquarters, especially the latter, are but feebly developed.

Both the live buffaloes in the National Museum collection of living animals are developing the same shortness of body and lack of muscle, and when they attain their full growth will but poorly resemble the splendid proportions of the wild specimens in the Museum mounted group, each of which has been mounted from a most careful and elaborate series of post-mortem measurements. It may fairly be considered, however, that the specimens taken by the Smithsonian expedition were in every way more perfect representatives of the species than have been usually taken in times past, for the simple reason that on account of the muscle they had developed in the numerous chases they had survived, and the total absence of the fat which once formed such a prominent feature of the animal, they were of finer form, more active habit, and keener intelligence than buffaloes possessed when they were so numerous. Out of the millions that once composed the great northern herd, those represented the survival of the fittest, and their existence at that time was chiefly due to the keenness of their senses and their splendid muscular powers in speed and endurance.

Under such conditions it is only natural that animals of the highest class should be developed. On the other hand, captivity reverses all these conditions, while yielding an equally abundant food supply.

**Questions:**

12. Which of the following, if true, most undermines the author's thesis?

    A. Not all captive bison developed the weak form described by the author.
    B. Some animals closely related to bison grow larger when kept in captivity.
    C. Wild bison who are underfed do not develop the same muscle tone as those who are not underfed.
    D. Bison who are idle in the wild look more like other wild bison than captive bison.
    E. Bison who are active in captivity look more like wild bison than other captive bison.

13. Which of the following, if true, would most undermine the author's thesis?

    A. A professional elephant hunter was well-known for his moving, poetic descriptions of the power and stature of elephants.
    B. A captive bison raised in the wild does not show any of the symptoms (small size, underdevelopment) described by the author.
    C. Bison raised at another zoo grew up to be short and underdeveloped.
    D. Professional bison hunters would often measure especially large animals they had killed for record keeping purposes.
    E. Immediately following the start of systematic bison hunting, unusually large and powerful individual bison died out, never to be seen again.

## Verbal Reasoning: Text Completion Task Simulation

1 - Despite her initial skepticism, Janet found the arguments in the article _____; she couldn't deny the strong evidence and logical reasoning presented.

A) unpersuasive
B) compelling
C) insignificant
D) irrelevant

2 - The once _____ marketplace had quieted down significantly in recent years, with many vendors moving online to find more lucrative sales environments.

A) bustling
B) stagnant
C) desolate
D) vibrant

3 - His approach to solving complex problems is highly _____, often involving multiple disciplines and perspectives that lead to innovative solutions.

A) traditional
B) interdisciplinary
C) straightforward
D) narrow

4 - The government's policy on immigration was criticized for being too _____, lacking the flexibility needed to address the nuances of individual cases.

A) lenient
B) rigid
C) accommodating
D) generous

5 - In her latest book, the historian offers a(n) _____ analysis of the social dynamics of medieval Europe, shedding light on previously overlooked aspects of daily life.

A) superficial
B) erroneous
C) insightful
D) biased

6 - The CEO's strategy for turning around the company was _____; rather than cutting costs, he focused on expanding into new markets.

A) cautious
B) counterintuitive
C) predictable
D) prudent

7 - The playwright's new work is a(n) _____ of modern society's obsession with technology, portraying its impact on human relationships through sharp dialogue and dynamic characters.

A) endorsement
B) critique
C) celebration
D) examination

8 - Environmental activists argue that the city's plan to build more roads is _____, likely leading to increased traffic rather than solving the congestion issue.

A) misguided
B) beneficial
C) inevitable
D) effective

9 - The lecture was intended to be _____, but due to the complex nature of the topic, many students found it confusing and difficult to follow.

A) comprehensive
B) introductory
C) entertaining
D) detailed

## Verbal Reasoning: Sentence Equivalence Task Simulation

1 - The CEO's plan to overhaul the company's marketing strategy was _____, given the recent downturn in sales and the need for a more dynamic approach.

A) unnecessary
B) pivotal
C) crucial
D) redundant
E) essential
F) optional

2 - The debate on environmental policy was _____, with experts from various fields providing diverse perspectives that enriched the discussion.

A) monotonous
B) multifaceted
C) singular
D) polarized
E) one-dimensional
F) varied

3 - His remarks on the new policy were _____, sparking debates among colleagues who either strongly supported or vehemently opposed his views.

A) innocuous
B) trivial
C) contentious
D) provocative
E) benign
F) stirring

4 - The artist's new exhibition is _____; it challenges conventional aesthetics and pushes the boundaries of traditional media.

A) derivative
B) innovative
C) groundbreaking
D) imitative
E) customary
F) standard

5 - Her approach to solving complex problems is highly _____, often involving a series of methodical steps that ensure thorough analysis and effective solutions.

A) haphazard
B) systematic
C) erratic
D) structured
E) random
F) orderly

6 - The recent legislative changes are _____, intended to streamline the process but instead complicating it further for most businesses.

A) clarifying
B) obfuscating
C) simplifying
D) enlightening
E) muddling
F) elucidating

7 - The historical novel's depiction of the era is _____, capturing the complexities and nuances of the time with remarkable accuracy and depth.

A) vague
B) simplistic
C) superficial
D) authentic
E) precise
F) accurate

8 - In his latest blog post, the author argues that modern cinema has become too _____, focusing more on visual effects than on narrative depth.

A) substantive
B) superficial
C) profound
D) shallow

E) meaningful
F) trivial

9 - Public reaction to the new urban policy has been _____, with some praising its vision and others decrying its impact on community dynamics.

A) uniform
B) divergent
C) homogeneous
D) mixed
E) consistent
F) varied

## Quantitative Reasoning: Quantitative Comparisons Task Simulation

Quantity A: The number of integer solutions to the equation $2x + 4 = 10$.
Quantity B: The number of integer solutions to the equation $3x - 9 = 0$.

Quantity A: The length of the diagonal of a square with a side of 5 cm.
Quantity B: The length of the side of a square with an area of 25 cm².

Quantity A: The product of the first four prime numbers.
Quantity B: 30

Quantity A: $\sqrt{100}$
Quantity B: The number of degrees in the interior angle of a regular pentagon.

Quantity A: The sum of the angles in a heptagon.
Quantity B: 900 degrees

Quantity A: $x$, where $x$ is the value that satisfies $log_2 (x) = 5$.
Quantity B: 30

Quantity A: The total surface area of a cube with an edge length of 3 cm.
Quantity B: The total surface area of a sphere with a radius of 3 cm. Use π = 3.14 and surface area formula 4πr².

Quantity A: The probability of flipping exactly two heads in three-coin tosses.
Quantity B: $\frac{1}{3}$


Quantity A: The maximum number of points where three distinct circles can intersect each other.
Quantity B: 6


## Quantitative Reasoning: Problem solving Task Simulation

1 - If $x$ is an integer such that $-2 \leq x \leq 5$, what is the maximum value of $2x - x^2$ ?


2 - A bookstore sells novels and biographies. If novels make up 40% of the total number of books and there are 120 more biographies than novels, how many books are there in total?


3 - A car travels from Town A to Town B at a speed of 60 km/h and returns from Town B to Town A at 80 km/h. What is the average speed for the round trip?


4 - In a mixture of coffee and chicory, the ratio of coffee to chicory is 5:3. If 8 kg of chicory is added to the mixture, the ratio becomes equal (1:1). How much coffee was in the original mixture?


5 - A rectangular garden measuring 20 meters in length and 15 meters in width is surrounded by a uniform path. If the area of the path is equal to the area of the garden, how wide is the path?


6 - An isosceles triangle has a perimeter of 36 cm. If each of the equal sides is three times the length of the base, find the length of the base.

7 - A set of numbers has an average of 50. If the largest number, 80, is removed, the average of the remaining numbers is now 45. How many numbers were in the original set?


8 - Water flows into a tank with a capacity of 150 liters through an inlet pipe that can fill it in 5 hours. If there is a leak that can empty the full tank in 10 hours, how long will it take to fill the tank?


9 - What is the sum of the series 2 + 5 + 8 + ... + 50?

10 - A 10-meters-long ladder leans against a wall. The bottom of the ladder is pulled away from the wall at a rate of 2 meters per second. How fast is the top of the ladder sliding down the wall when the bottom is 6 meters from the wall?

11 - A sphere is inscribed in a cube with a volume of 27 cubic meters. What is the volume of the sphere.

12 - Two trains, 360 meters and 240 meters long, are running on parallel tracks in opposite directions with speeds of 72 km/h and 54 km/h. How long will it take for the trains to completely pass each other?

13 - A digital clock displays hours and minutes from 00:00 to 23:59. How many times in a day does the digital display show consecutive numbers such as 01:23 or 12:34?

## Quantitative Reasoning: Data Interpretation Task Simulation

1 - Sectorial Profit Margins Over Time

Graph Type: Line Graph

Data Content: Annual profit margins for five sectors (Technology, Healthcare, Energy, Consumer Goods, Finance) over five years.

Question: Identify the sector with the most consistent increase in profit margin over the five-year period.

Choices:
A) Technology
B) Healthcare
C) Energy
D) Consumer Goods

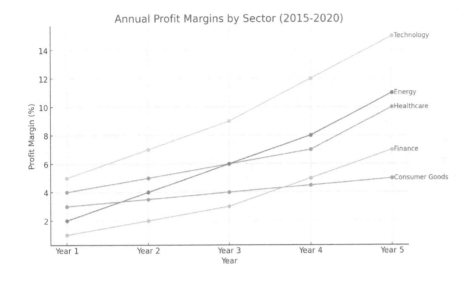

Annual Profit Margins by Sector (2015-2020)

2 - Investment Returns Over Time

Graph Type: Candlestick Chart

Data Content: Monthly investment returns for a portfolio of stocks, bonds, and commodities over the past year.

Question: Which investment type exhibited the highest variability in returns?

Choices:
A) Stocks
B) Bonds
C) Commodities
D) Returns are uniformly distributed across all investments

3 - Market Research Consumer Preferences

Graph Type: Box Plot

Data Content: Customer satisfaction ratings (scale of 1-10) across five product categories over four quarters.

Question: In which product category do customers show the most consistent satisfaction, indicated by the narrowest interquartile range?

Choices:
A) Product Category 1
B) Product Category 2
C) Product Category 3
D) Product Category 4

Customer Satisfaction Ratings Across Product Categories

4 - Production Costs Analysis

Graph Type: Area Graph

Data Content: Monthly production costs for raw materials, labor, and overhead in a manufacturing company throughout one year.

Question: Which cost component accounted for the greatest proportion of total production costs in the final quarter of the year?

Choices:
A) Raw materials
B) Labor
C) Overhead
D) They were approximately equal

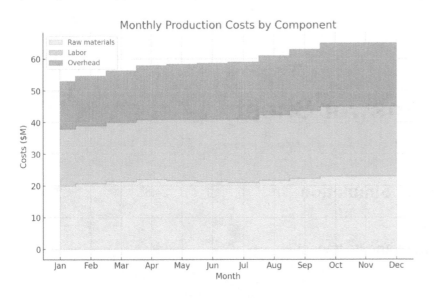

Monthly Production Costs by Component

5 - Comparison of Educational Expenditure

Graph Type: Bar Graph

Data Content: Annual spending on education per student in primary, secondary, and tertiary educational levels across four countries.

Question: Which country spends the most on tertiary education?

Choices:
A) Country L
B) Country M
C) Country N
D) Country O

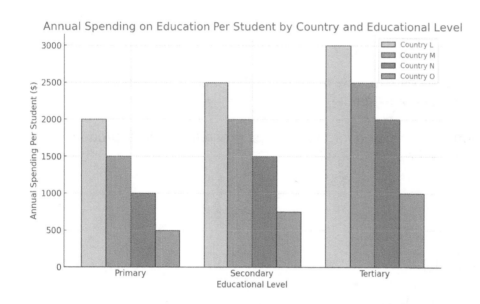

# Answer Sheet

## Analytical Writing: Issue Task Simulation

"Analyzing the Issue on Global Trade and Its Impact"

### Essay Planning Guide

## Introduction

Thesis Statement: Clearly articulate your stance on whether global trade is more beneficial or detrimental for developing and developed nations.
Example: "Global trade, despite its challenges, plays a pivotal role in the economic advancement of nations, offering benefits that outweigh its drawbacks."

## Body Paragraphs

1 Argument Supporting Your Thesis:
Main Idea: Detail the positive impacts of global trade on economic growth and development.
Example: Discuss the creation of jobs and access to markets that global trade provides for developing countries, using specific country data as evidence.

2 Counterargument and Rebuttal:
Main Idea: Acknowledge the potential negative impacts of global trade, such as economic dependency and exploitation.
Counterargument Example: Cite instances where global trade has led to economic destabilization or exploitation in certain regions.
Rebuttal Example: Argue that with proper regulatory frameworks, the benefits of global trade can be maximized while minimizing its negative effects.

3 Further Supporting Argument for Example:
Main Idea: Provide additional evidence on how global trade contributes to technological advancement and cultural exchange.
Example: Highlight how global trade has facilitated the spread of technology and cultural ideas across borders, enriching societies.

## Conclusion

Summary: Recapitulate the main arguments supporting the beneficial aspects of global trade.
Restatement of Thesis: Emphasize the overarching conclusion that global trade, while complex, is fundamentally beneficial when managed effectively.
Closing Thought: Offer a perspective on the future of global trade and its potential to further global cooperation and development.

**Evaluation Criteria** (For Review and Self-Assessment):

Clarity and Precision: Assess the clarity and precision of the thesis and arguments.
Coherence and Logic: Evaluate the logical flow and coherence of the essay.
Relevance and Support: Consider the relevance and robustness of the examples and evidence used.
Syntax and Grammar: Review the proficiency of language and grammatical accuracy.

This structured guide serves as an "answer sheet" for crafting a comprehensive and persuasive essay on the nuanced issue of global trade's impacts, providing a method to explore various facets of the issue methodically

# Verbal Reasoning: Reading Comprehension Task Simulation

1. **Correct Answer:** authoritative and assured

**Explanation:** The author's tone in this passage is authoritative and assured. You can tell is it authoritative because the author speaks with an academic and commanding voice. You can tell it is assured because the author leaves little room for debate or opposition; he does not question himself or relate the opposite sides of the debate to his argument. Rather, he states his points as if they are fact. Failing this approach, you could also eliminate the other answer choices for how they fail to capture the tone of the author.
The author could not be called "demanding" because although he is commanding in his use of language and his certainty, he is not urging the reader to make a change, but rather simply illuminating what he believes should happen with regard to words and names. You certainly could not call the author's tone
"nonchalant" or "ambivalent" because he clearly cares deeply about the subject matter. And, while the author might be a little bit haughty, he never approaches condescension.

2. **Correct Answer:** The definition of English words and phrases are often vague and debatable.

**Explanation:** This phrase is used very early in the passage, in the opening lines of the introduction. In context, the author states, "We cannot inquire far into the meaning of proverbs or traditional sayings without discovering that the common understanding of general and abstract names is loose and uncertain. Common speech is a quicksand." To best determine the answer, it is best to understand the introduction as it relates to the entire essay, as authors usually introduce the main point of their essay early in the introduction.
The primary point of the essay is to discuss the problems with ambiguity in the application of words and names, so when the author says that "common speech is a quicksand," it is reasonable to assume that he means common speech alters and varies the meanings of words rapidly to create words and phrases that are vague and debatable.

3. **Correct Answer:** If words and names are to mean the same thing to all people, then the meanings and implications of those words must be somehow conclusively determined.

**Explanation:** In the context in which the author uses this quotation, he is discussing the difference between what he defines as the "Logical Concept," which is when words and names have a defined meaning for all speakers, and the "Personal" and "Vernacular Concept," which is where words differ from individual to individual and social group to social group. It is clear from the author's tone and conclusions throughout the paragraph and passage that he believes a "Logical Concept" of words needs to exist in order for language to be universally applied and understood. From this conclusion, we can easily determine the meaning of the underlined text. He wishes to underscore the importance of having a fixed meaning for words and names so as to avoid error and confusion in speech. The correct answer best summarizes this meaning.

Some of the other answer choices might seem reasonable, but crucially, they are conclusions that the author reaches at different points in the essay. The answer choice "The meaning and connotation of names can be fixed, so that human intercourse will proceed without confusion and error" is incorrect because of the word "can"; the author is closer to saying it ought to be done, rather than it can be done. Likewise, the answer choice "It is of fundamental importance that the meaning of words and names be understood universally by all people to prevent debate and unnecessary arguments" is incorrect because the author does not mention debate and disagreement in this particular passage.

This is a difficult question to answer because so many of the answer choices seem like possible alternatives, but when tasked with deciphering the meaning of a certain excerpt, it is important to use the rest of the essay for context, but to also focus on the exact words the author uses when translating the correct answer.


4. **Correct Answer:** The Vernacular Concept varies by social group or generation, whereas the Personal Concept varies by individual.

**Explanation:** Answering this question requires you to read critically and understand the definitions attributed by the author to various terms he creates. In the third paragraph, he describes what he means by the Personal Concept and the Vernacular Concept, so it really is just a matter of reading carefully. Of the Personal Concept, the author says, "in actual speech we have also the Personal Concept, which varies more or less with the individual user," and of the Vernacular Concept, the author says,

"the Popular or Vernacular Concept, which, though roughly fixed, varies from social sect to social sect and from generation to generation."


5. **Correct Answer:** Our individual preconceptions blind us to the true meaning of words and prevent us from accurately penetrating the combined knowledge of humanity.

**Explanation:** The main point of the sixth paragraph is best captured in the following few sentences: "The accumulated wisdom of mankind is stored in language. Until we have cleared our conceptions, and penetrated to the full meaning of words, that wisdom is a sealed book to us. Wise maxims are interpreted by us hastily in accordance with our own narrow conceptions." Here, the author discusses how people's individual preconceptions blind them to the true meaning of words, and draws his conclusions on how this individual approach to definition and meaning prevents people from accessing to combined wisdom of humanity. The other answer choices either summarize the wrong paragraph, or else do not properly penetrate to the heart of the author's argument in this paragraph.


6. **Correct Answer:** We learn the meaning of most words organically and as a result the exact definition and application of those words will differ from person to person.

**Explanation:** The second paragraph begins with the author stating, "Consider how we acquire our vocabulary, how we pick up the words that we use from our neighbors and from books." We thus know that the second paragraph is going to be a consideration of how we acquire words and definitions for things. The author goes on to state, "We hear the words applied to individual objects; we utter them in the same connection; we extend them to other objects that strike us as like without knowing the precise points of likeness that the convention of common speech includes." This tells us that the author believes we learn words "organically," or naturally. Finally, the author says, "The individual's extension of the name proceeds upon what in the objects has most impressed him when he caught the word: this may differ in different individuals." This tells us that the author believes the result of our organic learning is that the exact definition and application of words differs from person to person. The other answer choices either summarize a small part of the paragraph, or else they draw incorrect conclusions from the author's writing.

7. **Correct Answer:** Disputes over which country's laws to apply in commercial trade situations can chill future trade arrangements with other countries, even those which belong to the CISG.

**Explanation:** Given that the purpose of CISG is to reduce disputes over trade between countries, the correct answer is, "Disputes over which country's laws to apply in commercial trade situations can chill future trade arrangements with other countries, even those which belong to the CISG." This is the correct answer because the inference can be made that if the CISC is reducing disputes between countries, and that there is a weaker chance of future trade arrangements being chilled.

8. **Correct Answer:** It would be to Rwanda's benefit to join the CISG.

**Explanation:** The correct answer is, "It would be to Rwanda's benefit to join the CISG."
A tempting wrong answer is "It is imperative that Rwanda join the
CISG in order to avoid impending trade disputes that could prove to be disastrous." However, this is not correct because the author does not take such an extreme position. While the author believes it would be in Rwanda's favor to join the CISG, there is no indication that the author foresees disastrous results if Rwanda foregoes joining.
The other answer choices state positions that are directly contrary to the author's arguments:
"The CISG has a narrow window of applicability," is wrong because the author argues that the CISG is broadly applicable.
"Although joining the CISG has benefits, Rwanda ultimately should not join the CISG," is wrong because the author states that Rwanda should join the CISG.
"There are positive and negative aspects that Rwanda should weigh and balance when deciding whether to join the CISG," is wrong because the author does not argue that Rwanda should weigh and balance positives and negatives, but rather states that Rwanda should simply join.

9. **Correct Answer:** provide an example that makes an abstract concept easier to understand

**Explanation:** The purpose of the second paragraph is to "provide an example that makes an abstract concept easier to understand." In fact, the second paragraph discusses the scenario of a trade arrangement between Uganda and China in order to show the practial applications of the CISG. The purpose of the second paragraph is also signaled in the last sentence of the first paragraph, which reads, "To help make this concept more tangible, consider the following hypothetical."

10. **Correct Answer:** To explain why Rwanda should become a member of the CISG

**Explanation:** The article is written with a heavy-handed favoritism towards Rwanda becoming a member of the CISG. This is especially apparent in the opening and closing paragraphs. Therefore, the correct answer is "Explain why Rwanda should become a member of the CISG."

11. **Correct Answer:** strong debate

**Explanation:** The phrase, "heated discussion" appears in the last paragraph in this sentence: "There has been heated discussion as to whether Rwanda should sign the CISG." Given the context in which the phrase appears, it seems to mean that strong arguments are being made both for and against membership in the CISG. As such, "strong debate" is the best answer, as the discoure is not emotional, is not characerized as being combative, nor unfair, and there is no indication that "intense persuasion" is being utilized.

12. **Correct Answer:** Bison who are idle in the wild look more like other wild bison than captive bison.

**Explanation:** The author's main explanation for why captive bison are smaller than normal and the bison in the Smithsonian collection are larger than normal hinges on the amount of exercise and activity animals living in both environments had. According to the author, wild bison living at the end of the bison hunts survived more chases and had more activity than was usual, meaning only the finest specimens survived, while captive bison were deprived of exercise and activity. Thus, if a wild bison that did not exercise and was not active looked more like other wild bison, some other factor besides exercise would have to be found to explain the difference in appearance between wild and captive bison.

13. **Correct Answer:** Immediately following the start of systematic bison hunting, unusually large and powerful individual bison died out, never to be seen again.

**Explanation:** The credited answer is the only one that addresses the author's central thesis - that the accounts and examples we have of bison are all in some way different from the norm of bison that existed in the wild-targeting his assumption that the mounted bison, being examples of the last, fittest survivors, are unusual in their size and fitness. If no unusually large bison had existed since the bison hunts first began, then it could not be possible that the last survivors of the bison hunts would be unusually large. Thus, the National Museum specimens he mentions could not be anomalous examples in the way he describes.

# Verbal Reasoning: Text Completion Task Simulation

1 - Despite her initial skepticism, Janet found the arguments in the article _____; she couldn't deny the strong evidence and logical reasoning presented.

**Answer**: B) compelling

**Explanation**: The context suggests that Janet was persuaded despite her doubts, so "compelling" fits as it describes something convincing and persuasive.

2 - The once _____ marketplace had quieted down significantly in recent years, with many vendors moving online to find more lucrative sales environments.

**Answer**: A) bustling

**Explanation**: "Bustling" describes a place full of busy activity, which contrasts with the current quiet state of the marketplace, highlighting the change over time.

3 - His approach to solving complex problems is highly _____, often involving multiple disciplines and perspectives that lead to innovative solutions.

**Answer**: B) interdisciplinary

**Explanation**: The mention of involving multiple disciplines directly supports "interdisciplinary," which refers to integrating different academic disciplines or fields.

4 - The government's policy on immigration was criticized for being too _____, lacking the flexibility needed to address the nuances of individual cases.

**Answer**: B) rigid

**Explanation**: "Rigid" means strict and inflexible, aligning well with the criticism for not accommodating individual case nuances.

5 - In her latest book, the historian offers a(n) _____ analysis of the social dynamics of medieval Europe, shedding light on previously overlooked aspects of daily life.

**Answer**: C) insightful

**Explanation**: "Insightful" suggests a deep and clear understanding of a complex topic, which is suitable here as it describes an analysis that brings to light new perspectives.

6 - The CEO's strategy for turning around the company was _____; rather than cutting costs, he focused on expanding into new markets.

**Answer**: B) counterintuitive

**Explanation**: "Counterintuitive" means against what one would intuitively expect; it fits here as expanding rather than cost-cutting is not the obvious choice in a turnaround strategy.

7 - The playwright's new work is a(n) _____ of modern society's obsession with technology, portraying its impact on human relationships through sharp dialogue and dynamic characters.

**Answer**: B) critique

**Explanation**: A "critique" is a detailed analysis and assessment of something, typically negative, making it the best choice given the context of portraying negative impacts.

8 - Environmental activists argue that the city's plan to build more roads is _____, likely leading to increased traffic rather than solving the congestion issue.

**Answer:** A) misguided

**Explanation**: "Misguided" means poorly conceived or incorrect in judgment, fitting the activists' view that the plan will not achieve its intended effect.

9 - The lecture was intended to be _____, but due to the complex nature of the topic, many students found it confusing and difficult to follow.

**Answer**: B) introductory

**Explanation**: "Introductory" implies a basic overview intended to introduce a topic, which aligns with the goal of simplicity, though it ended up being too complex for the students.

## Verbal Reasoning: Sentence Equivalence Task Simulation

1 - The CEO's plan to overhaul the company's marketing strategy was _____, given the recent downturn in sales and the need for a more dynamic approach.

**Answers**: C) crucial, E) essential

**Explanation**: Both "crucial" and "essential" indicate that the overhaul is vitally important and necessary, aligning well with the context of addressing a downturn in sales.


2 - The debate on environmental policy was _____, with experts from various fields providing diverse perspectives that enriched the discussion.

**Answers**: B) multifaceted, F) varied

**Explanation**: "Multifaceted" and "varied" both describe something with many aspects or features, suitable here as the debate was enriched by diverse expert perspectives.


3 - His remarks on the new policy were _____, sparking debates among colleagues who either strongly supported or vehemently opposed his views.

**Answers**: C) contentious, D) provocative

**Explanation**: Both "contentious" and "provocative" imply that his remarks incited strong reactions or debates, fitting the description of sparking division among colleagues.


4 - The artist's new exhibition is _____; it challenges conventional aesthetics and pushes the boundaries of traditional media.

**Answers**: B) innovative, C) groundbreaking

**Explanation**: "Innovative" and "groundbreaking" both suggest introducing new ideas or methods, which fits the context of an exhibition that challenges and pushes boundaries.


5 - Her approach to solving complex problems is highly _____, often involving a series of methodical steps that ensure thorough analysis and effective solutions.

**Answers**: B) systematic, D) structured

**Explanation**: Both "systematic" and "structured" describe an approach that is organized and methodical, appropriate for a process involving thorough analysis.


6 - The recent legislative changes are _____, intended to streamline the process but instead complicating it further for most businesses.

**Answers**: B) obfuscating, E) muddling

**Explanation**: "Obfuscating" and "muddling" both imply making something more confused or unclear, which matches the unintended consequence of complicating the process.

7 - The historical novel's depiction of the era is _____, capturing the complexities and nuances of the time with remarkable accuracy and depth.

**Answers**: D) authentic, F) accurate

**Explanation**: "Authentic" and "accurate" both denote a depiction that is true to reality, suitable for a novel that captures historical complexities with depth and precision.

8 - In his latest blog post, the author argues that modern cinema has become too _____, focusing more on visual effects than on narrative depth.

**Answers**: B) superficial, D) shallow

**Explanation**: Both "superficial" and "shallow" suggest a lack of depth, which aligns with the criticism that modern cinema focuses too much on visuals rather than narrative.

9 - Public reaction to the new urban policy has been _____, with some praising its vision and others decrying its impact on community dynamics.

**Answers**: D) mixed, F) varied

**Explanation**: Both "mixed" and "varied" describe a range of different reactions, fitting the description of diverse public opinions on the policy.

## Quantitative Reasoning: Quantitative Comparisons Task Simulation

Quantity A: The number of integer solutions to the equation $2x + 4 = 10$ (1 solution: $x = 3$).
Quantity B: The number of integer solutions to the equation $3x - 9 = 0$ (1 solution: $x = 3$).

**Answer**: The quantities are equal.

**Explanation**: Both equations simplify to one integer solution, $x = 3$ for both, hence they are equal.

Quantity A: The length of the diagonal of a square with a side of 5 cm ($\sqrt{5^2 + 5^2} = 5\sqrt{2} \approx 7.07$ cm).
Quantity B: The length of the side of a square with an area of 25 cm² (5 cm).

**Answer**: Quantity A is greater.

**Explanation**: The diagonal of a square (7.07 cm) is always longer than its side (5 cm) due to the Pythagorean theorem.

Quantity A: The product of the first four prime numbers (2, 3, 5, 7, which is 210).
Quantity B: 30

**Answer**: Quantity A is greater.

**Explanation**: The product of the primes (210) exceeds 30.

Quantity A: $\sqrt{100}$ (10).
Quantity B: The number of degrees in the interior angle of a regular pentagon ( $\frac{(5-2)x180}{5}$ =108 degrees).

**Answer**: Quantity B is greater.

**Explanation**: The value of $\sqrt{100}$ is 10, which numerically is less than 108 degrees.

Quantity A: The sum of the angles in a heptagon ((7 – 2) × 180 = 900 degrees).
Quantity B: 900 degrees

**Answer**: The quantities are equal.

**Explanation**: Both quantities calculate to 900 degrees.

Quantity A: x, where x is the value that satisfies $log_2$ (x) = 5 (32).
Quantity B: 30

**Answer**: Quantity A is greater.

**Explanation**: $log_2(x)$ = 5 gives x = $2^5$= 32, which is greater than 30.

Quantity A: The total surface area of a cube with an edge length of 3 cm (6 × $3^2$ = 54 cm²)
Quantity B: The total surface area of a sphere with a radius of 3 cm (4 × 3.14 × $3^2$ ≈ 113.04 cm²)

**Answer**: Quantity B is greater.

**Explanation**: The surface area of the sphere (113.04 cm²) is greater than that of the cube (54 cm²).

Quantity A: The probability of flipping exactly two heads in three-coin tosses ($\frac{3}{8}$).
Quantity B: $\frac{1}{3}$.

**Answer**: Quantity A is greater.

**Explanation**: The probability of two heads in three tosses (3 combinations out of 8 possible outcomes) is $\frac{3}{8}$, which is greater than $\frac{1}{3}$.

Quantity A: The maximum number of points where three distinct circles can intersect each other (6).
Quantity B: 6

**Answer**: The quantities are equal.

**Explanation**: Three circles can intersect at most at six different points if each pair of circles intersects at two points.

## Quantitative Reasoning: Problem solving Task Simulation

1 - Maximum value of $2x - x^2$ for $-2 \leq x \leq 5$:

**Explanation**: This is a quadratic equation, $y = -x^2 + 2x$, which opens downwards. Its vertex provides the maximum value. Vertex $x = -b/(2a) = -2/(2 \times -1) = 1$. Substituting $x = 1$ in the equation, $y = 2(1) - 1^2 = 1$.

**Answer**: The maximum value is 1 when $x = 1$.

2 - Total number of books in the bookstore:

**Explanation**: Let $n$ be the number of novels, so biographies are $n + 120$. Since novels are 40%, $\frac{n}{n+(n+120)} = 0.4$. Solving gives $n = 240$, and total books $n + n + 120 = 600$.

**Answer**: There are 600 books in total.

3 - Average speed for the round trip:

**Explanation**: Use the harmonic mean for average speed over equal distances: $\frac{2ab}{a+b}$ where $a = 60$ km/h and b=80 km/h. Calculation gives $\frac{2 \times 60 \times 80}{140} = 68.57$ km/h.

**Answer**: The average speed is approximately 68.57 km/h.

4 - Original amount of coffee in the mixture:

**Explanation**: Let coffee = $5x$ and chicory = $3x$. Adding 8 kg of chicory changes the ratio to 1:1, so $5x = 3x + 8$. Solving gives $x = 4$, coffee = 20 kg.

**Answer**: There were 20 kg of coffee in the original mixture.

5 - Width of the path around the garden:

**Explanation**: Let width be $w$. New total area (garden + path) = $(20 + 2w)(15 + 2w)$. Area of path equals area of garden: $300 + 70w + 4w^2 = 600$. *After some calculation we get* $2w^2 + 35w - 150 = 0$ Solving for $w$ gives $w = 3.5$ meters.

**Answer**: The path is 3.5 meters wide.

6 - Length of the base of the isosceles triangle:

**Explanation**: If the base is $x$ and equal sides are $3x$, perimeter $x + 2(3x) = 36$. Solving $x = 5.14$ cm.

**Answer**: The length of the base is 5.14 cm. (rounded to two decimal places)

7 - Number of numbers in the original set:

**Explanation**: Let $n$ be the number of numbers. Original sum = $50n$, new sum = $45(n - 1)$. Equate $50n - 80 = 45n - 45$, solving gives $n = 7$.

**Answer:** There were 7 numbers in the original set.

8 - Time to fill the tank with a leak:

**Explanation**: Filling rate = $\frac{1}{5}$ tank/hour, emptying rate = $\frac{1}{10}$ tank/hour. Net rate = $\frac{1}{5} - \frac{1}{10} = \frac{1}{10}$ tank/hour. Time to fill = $\frac{1}{\frac{1}{10}}$ = 10 hours.

**Answer**: It takes 10 hours to fill the tank.

9 - Sum of the series $2 + 5 + 8 + \ldots + 50$:

**Explanation**: This is an arithmetic series with first term 2, common difference 3. Last term 50, number of terms $n$ where $2 + (n - 1) \times 3 = 50$, solving gives $n = 17$.
Sum = $\frac{n}{2}$ (first+last) = $\frac{17}{2}$ (2+50) = 442.

**Answer**: The sum is 442.

10 - Rate at which the ladder top slides down the wall:

**Explanation**: Using related rates, $\frac{dx}{dt} = -2$ m/s at $x = 6$ m. $y^2 = 100 - x^2$, differentiating gives $2y\frac{dy}{dt} = -2x\frac{dx}{dt}$. Substitute and solve for $\frac{dy}{dt}$ when $x = 6$.

**Answer**: $\frac{dy}{dt} = -\frac{2\times6\times2}{2y}$, where $y = 8$. Thus, $\frac{dy}{dt} = -1.5$ m/s.
The top of the ladder is sliding down the wall at a rate of 1.5 meters per second when the bottom is 6 meters from the wall. The negative sign indicates that the height y is decreasing.

11 - Volume of the sphere inscribed in a cube:

**Explanation**: Cube side = $\sqrt[3]{27}$ = 3 meters, radius of sphere = $\frac{3}{2}$ meters.
Volume of sphere = $\frac{4}{3}$ πr³ = $\frac{4}{3}$π ( $\frac{3}{2}$ )³ = $\frac{9}{2}$ π cubic meters.

**Answer**: The volume of the sphere is $\frac{9}{2}$ π cubic meters.

12 - Time for trains to pass each other:

**Explanation**: Combined speed = 72 + 54 = 126 km/h = 126 × $\frac{1000}{3600}$ = 35 m/s. Total length = 360 + 240 = 600 meters. Time = $\frac{600}{35}$ seconds.

**Answer**: It takes about 17.14 seconds.

13 - Times consecutive numbers appear in a day:

**Explanation**: Possible combinations are 12:34, 01:23, 02:34, etc., appearing once every hour from 01:23 to 12:34.

**Answer**: They appear 12 times in a day.

# Quantitative Reasoning: Data Interpretation Task Simulation

1 - Analysis of Consistency in Growth:

Technology: Exhibits an increase in profit margin each year from 5% to 15%.
Healthcare: Also shows an increase each year, from 4% to 10%.
Energy: Profit margin grows every year from 2% to 11%.
Consumer Goods: Margin increases consistently though modestly, from 3% to 5%.
Finance: Shows growth each year, from 1% to 7%.
All sectors displayed a consistent increase in profit margins each year, with no declines over the period. To identify the sector with the most consistent increase:

Technology shows a consistent and substantial increase, making it a strong candidate for the sector with the most consistent increase over the period.
Given the data and the question posed, while all sectors increased consistently, Technology's increase was the most substantial in terms of percentage points added each year, thus fitting the criteria for "most consistent increase" both in terms of regularity and magnitude of growth.

**Correct answer:** A) Technology.

2 - Analysis:

Stocks show the greatest range between their monthly highs and lows, indicating significant variability.
Bonds have narrower high-low ranges, suggesting less variability.
Commodities also display considerable variability, but not as much as stocks.
The investment type with the greatest variability in revenue growth over the observed period, based on the maximum difference between high and low values each month, is Stocks. This matches the chart data and confirms A) Stocks as the answer to which industry shows the greatest volatility in revenue growth.

**Correct answer:** A) Stocks.

3 - Analysis:

Product Category 3 demonstrates the narrowest interquartile range (IQR) among the four categories, as observed from the compactness of its box plots across all quarters. This indicates a more consistent customer satisfaction rating.
Given that the interquartile range is the smallest for Product Category 3, it shows the most consistent customer satisfaction, indicated by the reduced variability in its satisfaction scores.

**Correct answer**: C) Product Category 3.

4 - Analysis for the Final Quarter:

Raw Materials: $23M in December, with progressive increases noted from October through December.
Labor: $22M in December, similarly increasing through the final quarter.
Overhead: $20M in December, showing a steady increase as well.
When reviewing the cumulative costs in the final quarter:
Raw Materials: $66M
Labor: $62M
Overhead: $55M

**Correct answer**: A) Raw materials


5 - From the graph and data analysis, it's evident that Country L spends the most on tertiary education among the four countries, with a spending amount of $3000 per student. This is the highest amount in the tertiary education category shown in the graph.

**Correct answer**: A) Country L

# CHAPTER 6: Additional Resources

## Essential GRE Vocabulary

Mastering the vocabulary component of the GRE is pivotal for excelling not just in the Verbal Reasoning section, but also for enhancing comprehension and expression throughout the test. The GRE is known for testing a broad range of advanced vocabulary, making a robust vocabulary foundation a critical part of preparation.

### Understanding GRE Vocabulary

The GRE targets academic and sophisticated lexicon that you're likely to encounter in graduate school rather than everyday conversation. This includes words that describe complex ideas and abstract concepts across various subjects such as the arts, sciences, and humanities. The aim is not just to test recognition but to examine the ability to apply this vocabulary in different contexts, ensuring that test-takers can understand and articulate complicated information effectively.

### Categories of Essential GRE Vocabulary

- **Abstract qualities:** Words that describe intangible and conceptual qualities such as "ephemeral," "taciturn," and "gregarious." These words often appear in Text Completion and Sentence Equivalence questions where nuanced understanding influences the choice of words.
- **Descriptive adjectives:** These adjectives are used to refine or clarify the meaning of nouns, essential for painting precise pictures in the reader's mind. Examples include "obdurate," "lucid," and "arduous."
- **Action verbs:** Verbs like "ameliorate," "bolster," and "mitigate" are frequently tested. They are powerful because they describe specific actions that can change the meaning of a sentence depending on the context.
- **Academic terms:** These are terms you might find in scholarly articles or discussions. Words such as "empirical," "anomalous," and "methodology" fall into this category.

### Strategies for Mastering GRE Vocabulary

- **Contextual learning:** Instead of rote memorization, learning words through context can help in understanding and remembering them better. Use new words in sentences, and read them in articles or books to see how they are used naturally.
- **Word lists:** Several GRE preparation books and online resources offer lists of the most commonly tested words on the GRE. These lists can be a good starting point, but

they should be used as part of a broader study plan that includes reading and exercises.

- **Prefixes, roots, and suffixes:** Understanding the building blocks of words can help you dissect unfamiliar vocabulary and make educated guesses when faced with unknown terms during the test.
- **Practice and usage:** Incorporate new vocabulary into everyday language or through writing exercises. Blogs, journals, or even social media captions can be useful platforms for practice.

### Applying Vocabulary in Practice Questions

Developing a strong vocabulary is not just about memorization but also about application. Regularly practice with GRE-style questions to test your ability to recognize and use vocabulary correctly. Sentence Equivalence and Text Completion questions, in particular, challenge you to apply your vocabulary knowledge in context, reinforcing your learning and improving your ability to make smart guesses based on word parts and context clues.

By expanding your vocabulary, you enhance your ability to express complex ideas clearly and accurately, a skill that is invaluable not only for the GRE but for success in graduate school and beyond. Thus, dedicated vocabulary building should be a cornerstone of your GRE preparation strategy.

# Vocabulary Exercises

To perform well on the GRE, it is essential to have a strong command of a wide range of advanced vocabulary. This section will explore effective vocabulary exercises designed to enhance your word power, crucial for excelling in the Verbal Reasoning section of the GRE. These exercises are tailored to build a robust vocabulary that is not only broad but deep, ensuring you understand the nuances of similar words and can distinguish between them in context.

## 1. Flashcards

Flashcards are a time-tested method for learning vocabulary. Start by creating flashcards for each new word, with the word on one side and its definition, part of speech, and an example sentence on the other. Regularly shuffle the flashcards and test yourself. For a digital approach, apps like Anki or Quizlet can provide spaced repetition algorithms that help optimize memory retention.

## 2. Daily Word Lists

Make a habit of learning and reviewing a set number of words each day. Many GRE prep resources provide lists of commonly tested words. Break these lists down into manageable daily goals. For instance, if you aim to learn 15 words per day, you could significantly expand your vocabulary in just a few months. Revisit these words regularly to ensure they move from short-term to long-term memory.

## 3. Contextual Reading

Incorporate reading into your study routine. Select articles from academic journals, quality newspapers, and magazines. Pay attention to new vocabulary and how it is used in context. This helps in understanding not just the definition of a word, but its connotations and typical usage.

## 4. Sentence Building

Practice using new vocabulary by writing sentences. This helps in cementing the words' meanings and uses in your mind. Challenge yourself further by writing short paragraphs or essays using a group of new words. This exercise is particularly useful for the Analytical Writing section of the GRE.

## 5. Vocabulary Games

Engage in word games like crosswords, word search, and scrabble, which are fun ways to learn new words. Online platforms and mobile apps offer GRE-specific vocabulary games that make learning engaging and competitive.

## 6. Synonyms and Antonyms

Understanding both synonyms and antonyms is crucial for the GRE, especially for questions that test your ability to discern slight differences in meaning. Create lists of synonyms and antonyms for each new word you learn, and quiz yourself on them.

## 7. Group Study and Peer Quizzes

Studying with peers can make the process more engaging. Try teaching new words to each other, and use them in discussions. You can also set up vocabulary quizzes and games, which are excellent ways to reinforce memory through social interaction.

## 8. Use Technology

Utilize technology to enhance your vocabulary training. Many websites and apps are designed specifically for GRE vocabulary preparation, offering exercises that include matching words to definitions, completing sentences, and more. These platforms often use algorithms to adapt to your learning level, increasing the difficulty as you improve.

## 9. Mnemonics

Create mnemonics to remember difficult words. Mnemonics are memory aids that help in encoding data into the memory in a way that is easier to recall. For example, the word "gregarious" (sociable) can be remembered with the phrase "Greg is always gregarious at gatherings."

## 10. Review and Reflect

Consistently review the words you've learned to solidify their meanings and uses. Reflection involves going beyond rote memory, considering how you might use these words in your everyday language or academic writing.

### 11. Application in Practice

The ultimate test of your vocabulary knowledge comes when you apply it to GRE practice questions. Regularly completing practice sections of the GRE that focus on Text Completion and Sentence Equivalence will help you understand how vocabulary is tested and allow you to apply what you've learned under test conditions.

By integrating these vocabulary exercises into your GRE preparation, you ensure that your vocabulary skills are robust and comprehensive, ready to tackle the challenges of the GRE and beyond.

# Math Review: Supplementary Math Exercises

1 - Complex Algebraic Equations:

Solve for x and y in the following system of equations:

$3x+4y = 10$
$2x^2 - y^2 = 6$

This exercise involves simultaneous equations with one being quadratic, testing algebraic manipulation skills.

2 - Advanced Geometry Problem:
A circle is inscribed in a triangle with sides measuring 8, 15, and 17. What is the radius of the inscribed circle.

This problem requires knowledge of the formula for the radius of an inscribed circle and tests the application of the Pythagorean theorem and triangle properties.

3 - Probability and Combinatorics:
A box contains 6 blue, 4 red, and 5 green balls. If three balls are picked at random, calculate the probability that they are all of different colors.

This exercise challenges the student's ability to calculate probabilities in a multi-event scenario.

4 - Data Interpretation with Functions:

Given the function $f(x) = 2x^2 - 15x^2 + 36x - 10$, determine the maximum value of $f(x)$ for x in the interval [1,10].

This exercise tests understanding of calculus concepts within a GRE context, focusing on the application of derivatives to find local maxima and minima.

5 - Statistics Problem:
From a set of numbers, the average (mean) is 15, and the standard deviation is 3.5. If one number is removed and the new mean becomes 14.5, find the removed number.

This problem assesses understanding of statistical measures and their implications on data sets.

6 - Trigonometric Identities:

Prove that $\tan(\alpha + \beta) = \frac{\tan \alpha + \tan \beta}{1 - \tan \alpha \tan \beta}$ using the sine and cosine addition formulas. This exercise tests knowledge of trigonometric identities and their derivations.

7 - Complex Number Manipulations:
Find the modulus and argument of the complex number $z = 1 - \sqrt{3i}$. This question challenges the student's ability to work with complex numbers, a topic that requires a good depth of understanding.

8 - Rate and Work Problem:
If Worker A can complete a task in 5 hours and Worker B can complete the same task in 3 hours, how long will it take for them to complete the task working together?

This classic problem tests the ability to analyze rates of work and combine them to find a collective rate.

9 - Logic and Set Theory:
Given sets A and B where |A|=10, |B|=15, and |A∩B|=5, find |A∪B|.

This problem tests understanding of set theory concepts, particularly with regard to union and intersection of sets.

10 - Optimization Problem:
A farmer has 2400 ft of fencing and wants to fence off a rectangular area that borders a straight river. He needs no fence along the river. What are the dimensions of the field that has the largest area? This problem is a classic optimization scenario that uses calculus to maximize the area function.

Implementation of Exercises
These exercises should be integrated into daily study routines as challenging practice problems. Students should attempt to solve these problems without a calculator where feasible to mimic GRE conditions, thereby enhancing their mathematical thinking and problem-solving speed. Regular review of concepts and formulas related to these exercises will help solidify understanding and improve performance on the actual exam.

# Answer Sheet with explanation

1 - Equations:

$3x+4y = 10$
$2x^2 - y^2 = 6$

**Solution**: First, solve the linear equation for y: $y = \frac{10-3x}{4}$. Substitute into the quadratic equation we will get a quadratic equation $23x^2 + 60x \ 196 = 0$ and solve for x. Substitute x values back into the expression for y.

**Answer**:

( x = 1.895, y = 1.079 ) and x = ( -4.5, y = 5.875 )

2 - Problem: A circle inscribed in a right triangle with sides 8, 15, and 17.

**Solution**: The area A of the triangle is $\frac{1}{2} \times 8 \times 15 = 60$. The semi-perimeter $s$ is $\frac{8+15+17}{2} = 20$. The radius $r$ of the inscribed circle is $\frac{A}{s} = \frac{60}{20} = 3$

**Answer**: Radius $r = 3$

3 - Problem: A box contains 6 blue, 4 red, and 5 green balls. If three balls are picked at random, calculate the probability that they are all of different colors.

**Solution**: Calculate the total number of ways to pick any three balls from the 15 available:

$\binom{15}{3} = 455$. Calculate the number of ways to pick one of each color:
$\binom{6}{1} \times \binom{4}{1} \times \binom{5}{1} = 6 \times 4 \times 5 = 120$. The probability is then $\frac{120}{455}$

**Answer**: Probability = $\frac{120}{455}$ = $\frac{24}{91}$ ≈ 0.2637

4 - Function: f(x) = 2x³ − 15x² + 36x − 10.

**Solution**: Calculate f ′ (x) = 6x² − 30x + 36. Set f ′ (x) = 0 and solve for x to find critical points. Test these in the second derivative or use a sign chart to determine maxima and minima.

**Answer**: Maximum at x = 10 with f(10) = 850.

5 - Problem: Find the removed number when the mean decreases after its removal.

**Solution**: Original mean of n numbers = 15. New mean of n − 1 numbers = 14.5. Total original sum = 15n, new sum = 14.5n − 14.5.
Removed number = 15n − (14.5n − 14.5) = 0.5n + 14.5. Assuming n = 2 and solving with given means leads to the number being 15.5.

**Answer**: Removed number = 15.5.

6 - Problem: Prove tan (α + β) = $\frac{tan\ \alpha + tan\ \beta}{1 - tan\ \alpha\ tan\ \beta}$

**Solution**: Use sine and cosine addition formulas to express sin(α + β) and cos(α + β), then divide the sine formula by the cosine formula and simplify.

**Answer**: Proof completed using identity transformations.

7 - Complex Number: number z = 1 − $\sqrt{3}i$

**Solution**: The modulus r is $\sqrt{1^2 + (-\sqrt{3})^2}$ = 2. The argument θ is found by $tan^{-1}(\frac{-\sqrt{3}}{1})$ .

**Answer**: Modulus = 2, Argument = $-\frac{\pi}{3}$

8 - Problem: Worker A and Worker B working together.

**Solution**: A's rate = $\frac{1}{5}$ , B's rate = $\frac{1}{3}$ . Combined rate = $\frac{1}{5} + \frac{1}{3} = \frac{8}{15}$ . Time taken working together = $\frac{15}{8}$ hours.

**Answer**: Time = 1.875 hours.

9 - Logic and Set Theory:

Problem: Calculate |A∪B|.

**Solution**: |A∪B| = |A| + |B| − |A∩B| = 10 + 15 − 5 = 20.

**Answer**: |A∪B| = 20

10 - Problem: Maximizing area of a rectangular field.

**Solution**: Perimeter minus river side = $2y + x = 2400$. Area A = $xy$. Maximize A = $x(\frac{2400-x}{2})$ and solve for $x$ using the derivative and set it equal to zero.

**Answer**: Dimensions: $x = 1200$, $y = 600$. Area = 720,000 square feet.

# Managing Test Anxiety

Test anxiety is a common challenge faced by many students preparing for high-stakes exams like the GRE. It can manifest as nervousness, worry, fear of failure, or even physical symptoms such as headaches or nausea. Managing test anxiety is crucial not only for improving performance but also for maintaining overall well-being during the preparation phase and on the test day. This section explores effective strategies and relaxation techniques to help mitigate anxiety and enhance focus and efficiency.

## Understanding Test Anxiety

Test anxiety typically stems from fear of negative evaluation, high personal expectations, or past experiences of poor performance. Recognizing the specific triggers of your anxiety is the first step toward managing it effectively. Once identified, you can employ targeted strategies to address these concerns.

## Cognitive Strategies

### Positive Reinforcement

Replace negative thoughts with positive but realistic affirmations. For example, change "I am bad at this" to "I am prepared and capable of handling this challenge."

### Visualization

Practice visualizing success. Spend time each day picturing yourself succeeding in your study sessions and feeling confident during the test.

## Goal Setting

Set clear, achievable goals for your study sessions. Breaking down your preparation into manageable tasks can reduce feelings of overwhelm and help build confidence as you achieve each goal.

## Behavioral Techniques

### Systematic Desensitization

Gradually expose yourself to the test environment. Start by simulating smaller portions of the test and gradually increase the test conditions' fidelity. This can reduce anxiety by making the test setting more familiar.

### Time Management

Develop a balanced study schedule. Avoid cramming by spreading your study sessions over a longer period. Regular breaks and free days are essential to prevent burnout.

### Mock Exams

Regularly take full-length practice tests under timed conditions. This not only helps with academic preparation but also conditions you to manage anxiety under simulated test conditions.

## Physical Techniques

### Deep Breathing Exercises

Learn and practice deep breathing techniques. Before and during the test, use deep breathing to manage acute anxiety and maintain focus. Simple techniques such as the 4–7–8 method (inhale for four seconds, hold for seven, and exhale for eight) can be particularly effective.

### Progressive Muscle Relaxation (PMR)

This involves tensing and then relaxing different muscle groups in your body. PMR can help alleviate physical symptoms of stress and anxiety that often accompany test-taking.

### Regular Physical Activity

Incorporate regular exercise into your routine. Physical activity can reduce stress levels, boost your mood, and improve your energy and concentration levels.

## Relaxation Techniques

### Mindfulness and Meditation

Practice mindfulness meditation to enhance your present-moment awareness, which can reduce racing thoughts and anxiety. Even short periods of meditation can be beneficial.

### Yoga

Yoga combines physical postures, breathing exercises, and meditation. It can be particularly effective in reducing stress and anxiety, improving your ability to concentrate and stay calm.

### Adequate Sleep

Ensure you get enough sleep during your preparation and especially before test day. Sleep is crucial for cognitive function and emotional regulation.

### Implementing the Strategies

To effectively manage test anxiety, integrate these strategies into your daily routine well ahead of the GRE. Regular practice will make these techniques more effective when you most need them, such as during an actual exam. Remember, the goal is to control anxiety so that it does not control you, enabling you to perform to the best of your ability.

By addressing both the mental and physical aspects of test anxiety, you can significantly improve your test performance and make your exam preparation journey a much more positive experience.

# Relaxation Exercises Before and During the Test

Preparing for a high-stakes test like the GRE can be stressful, and managing this stress is crucial for maximizing performance. Implementing relaxation exercises both before and during the exam can help reduce anxiety, improve concentration, and enhance overall test performance. This section outlines effective relaxation techniques that can be employed in the preparation phase and directly in the testing environment.

### Pre-Test Relaxation Techniques

### 1. Progressive Muscle Relaxation (PMR)

**Description:** Progressive Muscle Relaxation involves tensing each muscle group vigorously but without straining, then suddenly releasing the tension and noticing how the muscles feel when relaxed.

**Application:** Begin with your feet and work your way up to your face. This method not only helps reduce physical tension but also calms the mind.

**Timing:** Practice PMR during your study breaks and before going to bed the night before the test.

### 2. Deep Breathing Exercises

**Description:** Deep breathing helps control the nervous system and encourages the body to relax, bringing about a range of health benefits.

**Techniques:** Try diaphragmatic breathing, where you breathe deeply into your belly rather than your chest, or the 4–7–8 technique, which involves breathing in for four seconds, holding for seven, and exhaling for eight.

**Timing:** Integrate deep breathing into your daily routine and use it during study sessions, especially when you feel overwhelmed.

### 3. Guided Imagery

**Description:** This technique involves visualizing a peaceful scene to engage the mind in positive thoughts and distract it from anxieties.

**Application:** Close your eyes and imagine a place where you feel calm and relaxed, focusing on the sensory details of this place—the sights, sounds, and smells.

**Timing:** Practice guided imagery for a few minutes each day leading up to the test and especially the night before to ensure a restful sleep.

### Techniques for Use During the Test

### 1. Focused Breathing

**Description:** This involves paying close attention to your breathing pattern and consciously regulating it during stressful situations.

**Application:** Whenever you feel anxious during the test, pause for a moment, close your eyes, and take a few deep breaths to center yourself.

**Timing:** Employ focused breathing, especially before beginning the test, during breaks, and if you feel overwhelmed at any point.

### 2. Mini-Meditations

**Description:** Short meditation sessions can help reset your mind and improve focus.

**Technique:** Use simple mindfulness exercises, such as observing your thoughts without engagement or focusing intently on an object like a pencil or the desk surface.

**Timing:** Utilize mini-meditations during the test if you need to regain concentration or between different sections of the exam.

### 3. Quick Body Scans

**Description:** This involves a mental scan of your body for areas of tension, consciously releasing it.

**Application:** Start from the top of your head and move down to your toes, noticing any areas of tightness or discomfort and allowing them to relax.

**Timing:** Conduct quick body scans during breaks or when switching between test sections to alleviate physical discomfort and mental fatigue.

### 4. On-the-Spot Stretching

**Description:** Gentle stretching can relieve muscle tension and improve blood circulation, which is essential for maintaining energy and focus.

**Application:** Perform seated stretches targeting the neck, shoulders, arms, and legs.

**Timing:** Use stretching exercises during breaks or when you feel physically stiff during the exam.

### 5. Positive Affirmations

**Description:** These are short, positive statements that can help combat negative thoughts and set a positive mental attitude.

**Application:** Repeat affirmations such as "I am calm and focused" or "I am prepared and capable."

**Timing:** Whisper or mentally recite these affirmations before the test begins or during challenging moments throughout the exam.

Incorporating these relaxation exercises into both your test preparation and your test-taking strategy can significantly help manage anxiety and improve your overall performance. Regular practice of these techniques makes them more effective when you most need them, ensuring that you are both mentally and physically prepared for the demands of the GRE.

# CHAPTER 7: Beyond the GRE

## Planning Your Graduate School Application: Timeline

Applying for graduate school is a meticulous process that requires careful planning and organization. A well-thought-out timeline can alleviate stress and help ensure that all parts of your application are completed thoroughly and submitted on time. Here's a detailed guide on how to effectively plan your application process over the course of 12 to 18 months before your intended start date.

**18 to 12 Months Before Application Deadlines**

### Research and Decision-Making

**Start early:** Begin by researching potential graduate programs that align with your academic interests and career goals. Consider factors like faculty interests, program curriculum, location, size, cost, and available resources.

**Attend info sessions and webinars:** Many universities hold informational sessions both online and on campus. These can provide valuable insights into the program and offer networking opportunities with faculty and current students.

### Prepare for the GRE

**Study schedule:** Set up a realistic study schedule based on your diagnostic test results. Allocate more time to areas where you need the most improvement.

**Register for the test:** Choose an optimal time to take the GRE, allowing for retests if necessary. Ideally, plan to take the GRE at least ten months before your application deadlines to avoid any last-minute rush.

**12 to 9 Months Before Application Deadlines**

### Visit Schools

**Campus visits:** If possible, visit campuses to get a feel for the environment and meet with admissions representatives, faculty, and students. These visits can provide a deeper insight into the academic life and culture of the institution.

### Letters of Recommendation

**Identify recommenders:** Choose faculty or professional contacts who know you well and can attest to your academic or professional capabilities. It's crucial to choose people who can provide detailed and personal insights into your qualifications.

### *Draft Your Statement of Purpose*

**Start drafting:** Begin drafting your statement of purpose. This should be tailored to each program, highlighting your academic achievements, research interests, and how they align with the program's strengths.

## 9 to 6 Months Before Application Deadlines

### *Refine Application Materials*

**Edit rigorously:** Refine your statement of purpose and update your resume or curriculum vitae. Pay special attention to how these documents present your narrative and qualifications.

**Feedback:** Seek feedback on your application materials from mentors, advisors, or peers who are familiar with the application process.

### *Finalize Letters of Recommendation*

**Follow-up:** Remind your recommenders of the deadlines and provide them with all necessary forms and information to submit their letters.

## 6 to 3 Months Before Application Deadlines

### *Submit Applications*

**Early submission:** Aim to submit your applications as early as possible. This shows eagerness and ensures that any technical issues do not jeopardize your application.

**Keep copies:** Maintain personal copies of all parts of your application. Confirm that all components, including test scores and letters of recommendation, have been received by each program.

### *Financial Aid and Scholarships*

**Research funding options:** Look into scholarships, fellowships, and assistantship opportunities. Some applications for funding may be due at the same time as your program applications.

## 3 Months to Deadline

### *Follow-Up and Interviews*

**Check status:** Regularly check the status of your applications to ensure everything is processed correctly.

**Prepare for interviews:** Some programs may require interviews. If applicable, prepare thoroughly, focusing on discussing your research interests and how they align with the program's offerings.

*Stay Organized and Positive*

**Track responses:** Keep a log of the schools from which you have received responses. Prepare for possible rejections and remain positive as acceptances begin to come in.

Creating a detailed timeline for your graduate school applications helps in managing the extensive requirements efficiently. It ensures that you give yourself the best possible chance of success by being thorough and timely with each step of the process. Remember, the key to a successful application lies in early preparation and consistent follow-through.

# Choosing the Right Program

Selecting the right graduate program is a critical decision that can significantly influence your academic and professional future. It requires thorough research and introspection about your career goals, academic interests, and personal preferences. Here's a detailed guide on how to approach the process of choosing the best graduate program for your needs.

## Understand Your Academic and Career Objectives

### Clarify Your Goals

Begin by defining your long-term career objectives. Are you aiming to enter academia, research, industry, or a specific profession? Understanding your career path will help you identify the programs that best align with your aspirations.

Consider how different programs will enhance your skills, knowledge, and marketability in your chosen field.

## Research Programs Thoroughly

### Academic Strengths and Curriculum

Look into the curriculum and specialization options of potential programs. Ensure they align with your interests and goals.

Investigate the faculty profiles to assess their expertise, research interests, and their alignment with your academic objectives. Faculty mentorship is crucial in graduate studies, so find a program where you have potential mentors.

## Reputation and Accreditation

Check the program's reputation in the academic community and its ranking in your field of interest. Although rankings aren't everything, they can provide a general sense of a program's prestige and the quality of education.

Ensure the program is properly accredited, which affirms that it meets certain academic standards.

## Consider Practical Factors

### *Location*

Consider the geographical location of the institution. Think about whether you prefer an urban or rural setting, the climate, the cost of living, and proximity to significant industry hubs, which can be crucial for internships and job placements.

## Duration and Schedule

Assess the duration of the program. Some programs offer accelerated paths or part-time options that might better suit your personal circumstances.

## Cost and Financial Aid

Evaluate the total cost of the program, including tuition, fees, and living expenses. Research available financial aid options like scholarships, fellowships, grants, and assistantship opportunities that can offset some of the costs.

## Evaluate Student Life and Resources

### *Campus Resources*

Look at the resources available to graduate students, including libraries, laboratories, tech support, and career services. These resources can significantly enhance your academic experience and support your research or career development.

## Student Support Services

Consider the support services available for students, such as counseling, health services, and academic advising. A supportive environment can make a big difference in your graduate school experience.

## Community and Networking

Assess the community and networking opportunities within the program. Alumni networks, professional clubs, and academic organizations can provide crucial career support and networking opportunities post-graduation.

## Attend Open Houses and Reach Out

### *Visit and Engage*

If possible, visit the campuses of the programs you are considering. Attend open houses, tour facilities, and meet with admissions representatives, faculty, and current students. These visits can provide invaluable insights into the academic environment and student life.

**Reach Out to Current Students and Alumni**

Contact current students and alumni to get their perspectives on the program. They can offer honest feedback about the pros and cons of the program and provide details on how it has shaped their careers.

**Decision-Making**

*Compare and Decide*

After gathering all the necessary information, compare your top choices based on how well they match your academic needs, career goals, financial situation, and personal preferences.

Weigh the pros and cons carefully, considering both the short-term implications of your studies and the long-term impact on your career.

Choosing the right graduate program is an exercise in aligning your academic pursuits with your personal and professional aspirations. It requires diligent research and thoughtful consideration of a multitude of factors. By thoroughly evaluating each program against your goals and needs, you can make an informed decision that sets the stage for future success.

# Interpreting Your Score

Understanding your GRE scores is crucial for assessing how well you might fit into the graduate programs of your choice and for improving your study strategies if you plan to retake the test. The GRE General Test measures your verbal reasoning, quantitative reasoning, analytical writing, and critical thinking skills—all of which are fundamental for success in a wide range of graduate programs.

**Understanding the GRE Score Structure**

The GRE General Test comprises three main sections: Verbal Reasoning, Quantitative Reasoning, and Analytical Writing. Each of these sections is scored differently:

**1–2 Verbal and Quantitative Reasoning**

Both these sections are scored on a scale from 130 to 170, in one-point increments. The scores are based on the number of correct responses, which means there is no penalty for guessing.

Your raw score (the number of questions you answered correctly) is converted into a scaled score through a process called equating. This process adjusts for minor variations in difficulty among different test editions as well as the sections you might face.

## 3 Analytical Writing

This section is scored on a scale from 0 to 6, in half-point increments. The essay is scored by at least one human rater and a computer program called e-rater. If the scores from the human rater and e-rater are close, the average of these scores becomes the final score for the essay. Otherwise, a second human scores the essay, and the final score is the average of the two human scores.

## How to Interpret Your GRE Scores

### Benchmarking Against Program Requirements

Most programs publish the average GRE scores of their incoming classes. Comparing your scores with these averages can give you a good indication of where you stand. If your scores are well above the program's averages, you're in a strong position. If they're close, you're likely competitive. If they're lower, you might need to strengthen other areas of your application or consider how you might improve your scores on a retake.

### Understanding Percentiles

Alongside your scaled scores, you'll also receive percentile ranks. These ranks represent the percentage of test-takers who scored lower than you did. For example, if your percentile rank is 75, you scored higher than 75% of test-takers. High percentile ranks in the sections most relevant to your intended field of study can be particularly persuasive to admissions committees.

### Analytical Writing Insights

The scores for the Analytical Writing section reflect your critical thinking and analytical writing skills. They can be a critical factor in admissions, especially for programs that demand strong writing abilities. A score of 4.5 or above is generally considered good, but some highly competitive programs might look for even higher scores.

### Using Scores for Application Strategy

### Highlighting Strengths

If you have particularly strong scores in one section, consider how you might highlight this in your application. For example, a high quantitative score can be a selling point for engineering or science programs.

### Addressing Weaknesses

If your scores are lower in one area, think about how you can address this in your application. This might involve taking additional courses to prove your ability in that area or explaining the context of the score in your personal statement.

**Deciding on a Retake**

If you believe you can significantly improve your scores, retaking the GRE might be a good option. Many students score higher the second time around due to reduced anxiety and increased familiarity with the exam.

Understanding and effectively interpreting your GRE scores are essential for making informed decisions about your graduate school applications. It helps you realistically assess your chances of admission, tailor your application strategy, and decide if you need to retake the test to improve your chances.

# APPENDICES

## Common Pitfalls and How to Avoid Them

Achieving success on the GRE requires more than just understanding the material; it also involves strategic test-taking. Many test-takers, however, fall into common traps that can prevent them from reaching their full potential. This section outlines frequent pitfalls encountered during the GRE and provides practical strategies to avoid them.

### Pitfall 1: Poor Time Management

**Problem:** Running out of time can force you to rush through questions or, worse, leave them unanswered. This often occurs because test-takers spend too much time on challenging questions or fail to pace themselves appropriately.

**Solution:** Practice pacing in your study sessions. Use a timer to get accustomed to the amount of time you can spend on each question. During the test, if you're stuck on a question, make an educated guess, mark it for review if time allows, and move on. Always aim to have a few minutes in reserve to review and ensure all questions are answered.

### Pitfall 2: Overlooking Instructions

**Problem:** Misreading or skipping instructions can lead to incorrect answers, especially on the GRE where questions may be presented in complex formats.

**Solution:** Always read question instructions carefully. During your preparation, practice by paying close attention to the details of each question. Getting familiar with common question types and their instructions can also reduce the likelihood of making this mistake.

### Pitfall 3: Stress and Test Anxiety

**Problem:** High stress and anxiety can significantly impair your ability to focus and think clearly, leading to poor performance even if you're well-prepared.

**Solution:** Implement stress management techniques such as deep breathing or mindfulness meditation before and during the test. Regular exercise and a good night's sleep before the test day can also help reduce anxiety levels. During the test, take brief mental breaks if you feel overwhelmed.

### Pitfall 4: Relying on Memorization Over Understanding

**Problem:** Relying solely on rote memorization of formulas and vocabulary can be detrimental if the test questions require applying those concepts in unfamiliar contexts.

202

**Solution:** Focus on understanding concepts rather than just memorizing them. Use practice problems to apply these concepts in various scenarios, which helps deepen your understanding and ability to recall under pressure.

### Pitfall 5: Careless Errors

**Problem:** Simple mistakes such as calculation errors or misreading data can lead to incorrect answers, impacting your score negatively.

**Solution:** Develop a habit of double-checking your work, especially in the quantitative section. Practice making quick mental calculations accurately, and always review your answers if time permits.

### Pitfall 6: Inadequate Review of Weak Areas

**Problem:** Neglecting to strengthen weak areas can leave you vulnerable on test day, as the GRE is comprehensive and tests a wide range of skills.

**Solution:** During your preparation, use practice tests to identify your weak areas. Allocate more time to these areas and seek resources or help if necessary. Understanding why you got an answer wrong is just as important as practicing correct ones.

### Pitfall 7: Mismanaging the Computer-Adaptive Test Format

**Problem:** The computer-adaptive nature of the GRE means that the difficulty of questions adjusts based on your performance. Some test-takers become discouraged if they perceive the questions are becoming more challenging, which can affect their performance.

**Solution:** Understand that encountering tougher questions can be a sign that you're doing well. Maintain a steady approach regardless of the perceived difficulty of the questions. Stay confident and focus on answering each question to the best of your ability.

### Pitfall 8: Insufficient Practice Under Real Conditions

**Problem:** Practicing without mimicking the test conditions can lead to surprises and discomfort during the actual test.

**Solution:** Simulate real testing conditions during practice sessions. This includes following the exact time limits, using appropriate materials, and taking the full-length practice tests in a single sitting. Familiarity with the test format and conditions can greatly ease test-day stress.

By being aware of these common pitfalls and actively working to avoid them, you can improve your performance on the GRE. Effective preparation, combined with strategic test-taking, will enhance your ability to achieve a high score.

# Frequently Asked Questions

### What Is the GRE?

The Graduate Record Examination (GRE) is a standardized test that is an admissions requirement for many graduate schools in the United States and Canada. The GRE aims to measure verbal reasoning, quantitative reasoning, analytical writing, and critical thinking skills that have been developed over a long period of learning.

### How Is the GRE Scored?

The GRE consists of three main parts: Verbal Reasoning, Quantitative Reasoning, and Analytical Writing. The Verbal and Quantitative Reasoning sections are scored on a scale of 130–170, in one-point increments. The Analytical Writing section is scored on a scale from 0 to 6, in half-point increments. Scores are determined by your correct answers (known as the "raw score") and are then converted to the scaled score through a process called equating.

### How Often Can I Take the GRE?

You can take the GRE once every 21 days, up to five times within any continuous rolling 12-month period (365 days). This applies even if you canceled your scores on a test taken previously.

### What Is a Good GRE Score?

A "good" GRE score is one that gets you into your program of choice. Each graduate program has different requirements and expectations, so it's crucial to research the average scores at the schools to which you are applying.

### How Can I Prepare for the GRE?

Effective preparation typically involves reviewing content in the three test sections, practicing with sample questions, and taking full-length practice tests under timed conditions. Many students also benefit from using preparation books, online resources, or enrolling in a preparation course. It is also beneficial to focus on areas of weakness identified through initial practice tests.

### Can I Use a Calculator on the GRE?

Yes, you can use a calculator in the Quantitative Reasoning section of the GRE. However, it's a basic on-screen calculator, which is provided in the test interface for the computer-delivered test. For the paper-based test, a handheld calculator is provided at the test center.

### How Do I Send My GRE Scores to Schools?

After you take the GRE, you can send your scores to up to four graduate programs or business schools using the Score Select option, which is included in your test fee. You can also send scores to additional schools for a fee. You can choose which test scores to send to schools: your most recent score, all scores from the last five years, or any specific test administration from the last five years.

## What If I Need to Reschedule or Cancel My GRE Test?

You can reschedule or cancel your GRE test registration up to four days before your test date. A fee may apply. If you cancel your test, you may be eligible to receive a partial refund.

## Is the GRE Only for Prospective Graduate Students?

While the GRE is primarily used for admissions to graduate schools, including business and law programs that accept the GRE General Test in lieu of other exams, it is also used by some fellowships and grants for eligibility purposes.

## How Long Are My GRE Scores Valid?

GRE scores are valid for five years after the testing year in which you took the exam (i.e., until the end of the fifth year following your test year).

## What Does the GRE Test Measure?

The Graduate Record Examination (GRE) is designed to assess general academic readiness for graduate-level work. The test measures skills in three main areas: Analytical Writing, Verbal Reasoning, and Quantitative Reasoning. These areas evaluate critical thinking, analytical writing skills, quantitative problem-solving abilities, and reading comprehension widely used in graduate and business school programs.

## How Do I Register for the GRE?

You can register for the GRE online, by phone, or by mail. The easiest way is online through the ETS website where you can create an account, select your test date and location, and pay the registration fee. Be sure to register early to secure your preferred testing location and date.

## Can I Take the GRE at Home?

Yes, the GRE is available to be taken at home in most locations around the world, except Mainland China and Iran. The at-home test is monitored online by a proctor through ProctorU®. This option requires specific technical requirements, including a suitable computer, camera, and a stable internet connection.

## What Study Resources Are Recommended for the GRE?

A variety of resources are available for GRE preparation:

- **Official ETS material:** ETS provides several preparation materials, including *The Official Guide to the GRE General Test*, *GRE Practice Tests*, and the *ScoreItNow! Online Writing Practice*.

- **Third-party books and courses:** Many reputable companies offer books, classes, and online resources that include practice questions and tests.
- **Free online resources:** Various educational platforms offer free tutorials, sample questions, and tests that can be beneficial for understanding the exam format and practicing specific skills.

## How Should I Decide Which Graduate Programs to Send My Scores To?

Before selecting which programs to send your scores to, research each program thoroughly to understand their score requirements and how they fit with your academic and career goals. Consider programs where your scores align with or exceed the median scores of recently admitted students. Utilize the ETS ScoreSelect option to send the best scores that strengthen your application.

## What Are the Typical Mistakes to Avoid on the GRE?

Common mistakes include:

- Failing to manage time efficiently across sections, leading to unfinished questions.
- Overlooking simpler solutions to quantitative problems by not breaking down the question properly.
- Not structuring essays effectively in the Analytical Writing section, impacting clarity and coherence.

## How Important Are GRE Scores Compared to Other Application Components?

While GRE scores are an important component of most graduate school applications, their relative importance can vary significantly between programs. Some programs may emphasize work experience, academic transcripts, letters of recommendation, and personal statements more heavily. Always check with specific programs to understand how they weigh each component of the application.

## How Can I Improve My GRE Scores if I'm Not Satisfied?

If your initial scores aren't satisfactory:

- Analyze your performance to identify weaknesses.
- Adjust your study plan to focus more on these areas.
- Consider a prep course or tutor if self-study isn't effective.
- Practice under timed conditions to enhance your test-taking speed and accuracy.

## Are There Accommodations Available for Test-Takers with Disabilities?

Yes, ETS provides accommodations for test-takers with disabilities. These accommodations might include additional testing time, extra breaks, or the use of a computer for the Analytical Writing section. Applicants need to apply for accommodations in advance with appropriate documentation to support their requests.

## What Happens if I Need to Cancel My GRE Test Appointment?

If you need to cancel your GRE test, you can do so through your ETS account. Depending on when you cancel, you may be eligible for a partial refund. However, it's important to review the cancellation policy as fees and refund eligibility may vary.

Understanding these FAQs can help demystify the GRE and the application process, aiding candidates in their preparation and strategic planning. For further details, it is advisable to consult the official GRE website and the admissions offices of the prospective graduate programs.

13261329R00116